THE ODD

BY ALLAN PLENDERLEITH

ℛℛ
RAVETTE PUBLISHING

**THE ODD SQUAD and all related characters © 2004
Created by Allan Plenderleith**

All rights reserved.

First Published in 2004
Reprinted 2005
Ravette Publishing Limited
Unit 3, Tristar Centre, Star Road, Partridge Green, West Sussex RH13 8RA

Printed in Malta

ISBN: 1 84161 218 9

AS JEFF WALKED INTO THE ROOM HE HAD A FUNNY FEELING HIS MUM AND DAD HAD JUST BEEN UP TO SOMETHING

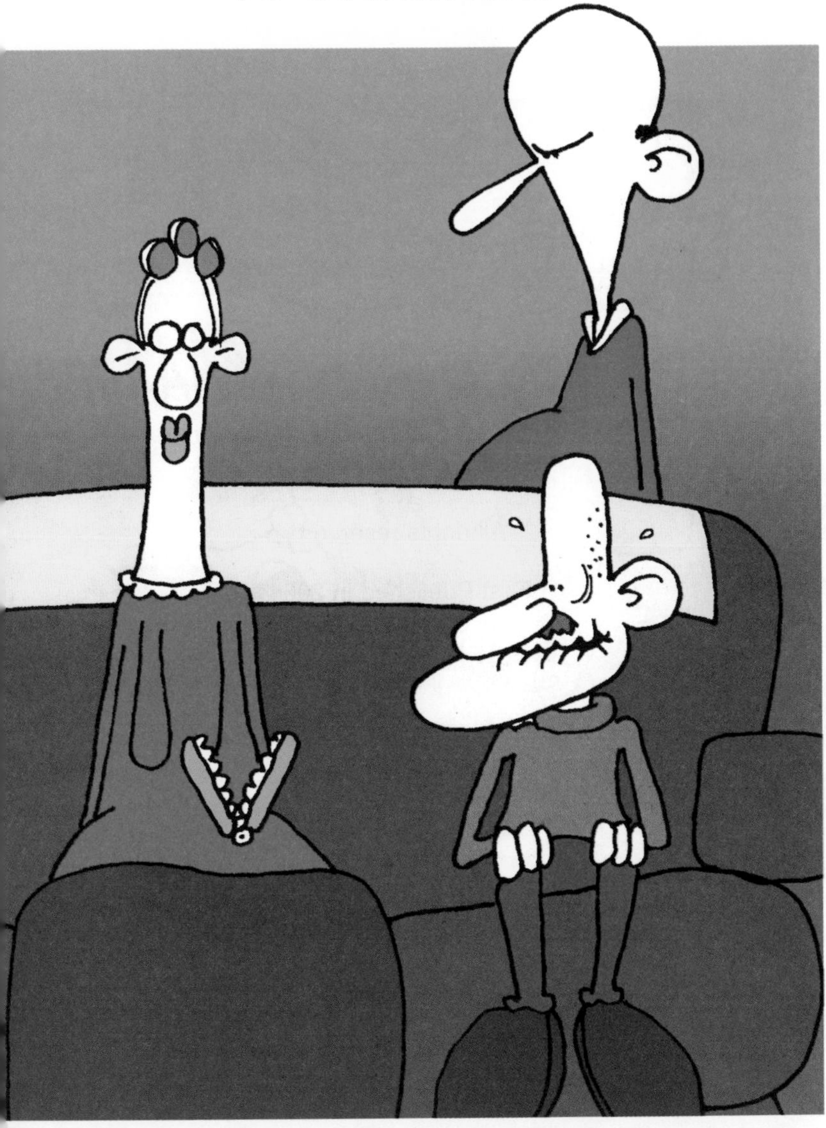

LILY LIKES TO SCARE THE LOCAL CHILDREN BY PAINTING AN EXTRA MOUTH ON HER DOUBLE CHIN

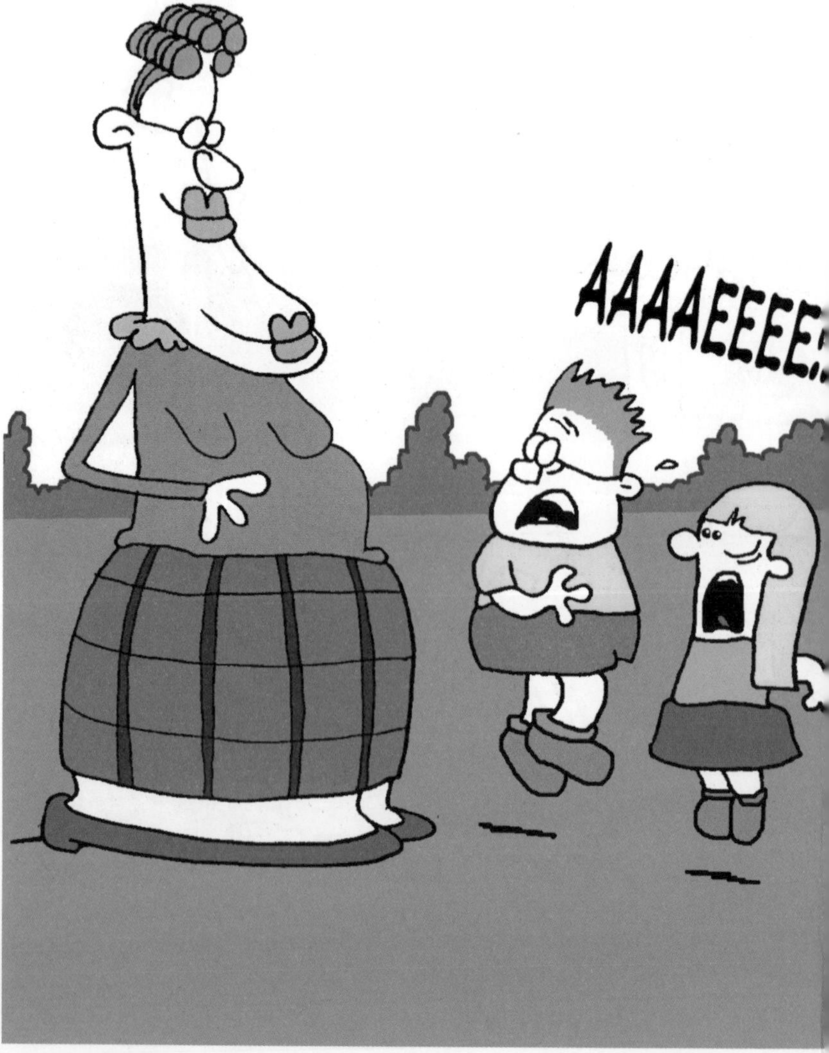
AAAAEEEE!

ALF TREATS LILY TO A SPECIAL PERFUME FOR OLDER LADIES

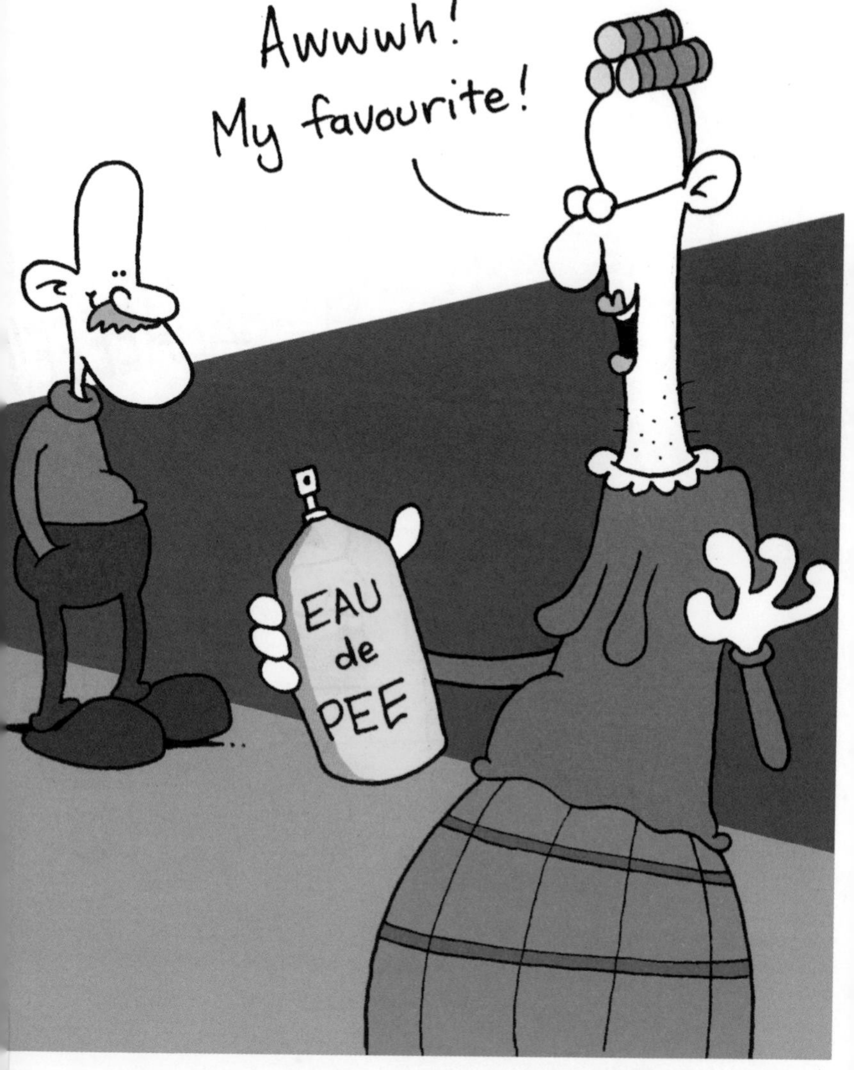

Awwwh! My favourite!
EAU de PEE

You know you're OLD when...

1. INSTEAD OF NIGHT CLUBS YOU GO TO CRAFT CLUBS!

CROCHET FOR BEGINNERS

2. YOU FEEL A STRONG GRAVITATIONAL PULL WHEN WALKING PAST GARDEN CENTRES!

GARDEN CENTRE

3. YOUR FRIDAY NIGHT ISN'T COMPLETE WITHOUT 'GROUND FORCE' OR 'CHANGING ROOMS'!

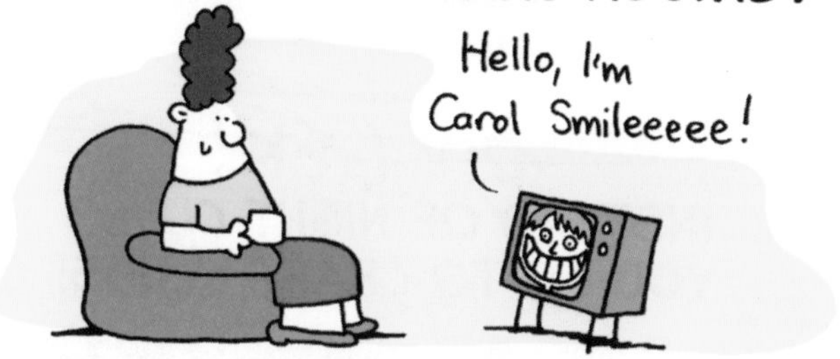
Hello, I'm Carol Smileeeee!

4. WHEN YOU STAND FROM A KNEELING POSITION THERE IS A LOUD NOISE

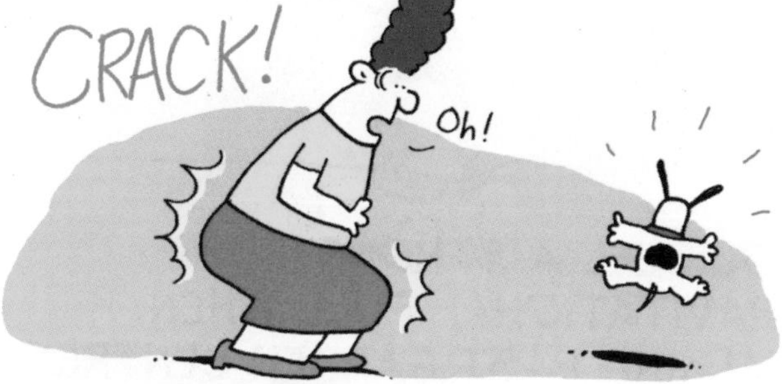
CRACK!
Oh!

5. YOU BEGIN SPROUTING HAIRS IN THE STRANGEST OF PLACES

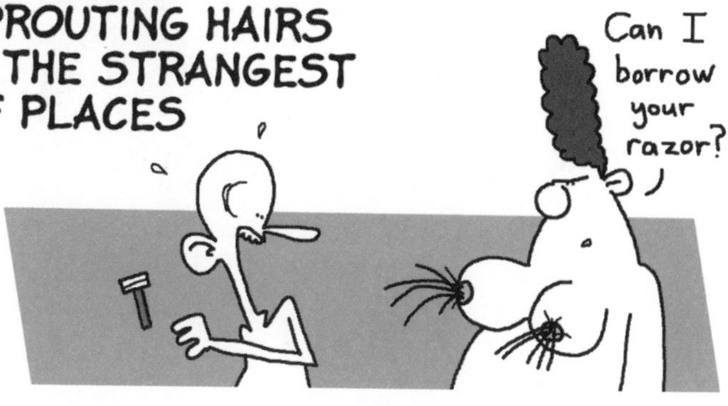
Can I borrow your razor?

IN HIS OLD AGE,
ALF GOT INTO CROSSWORDS

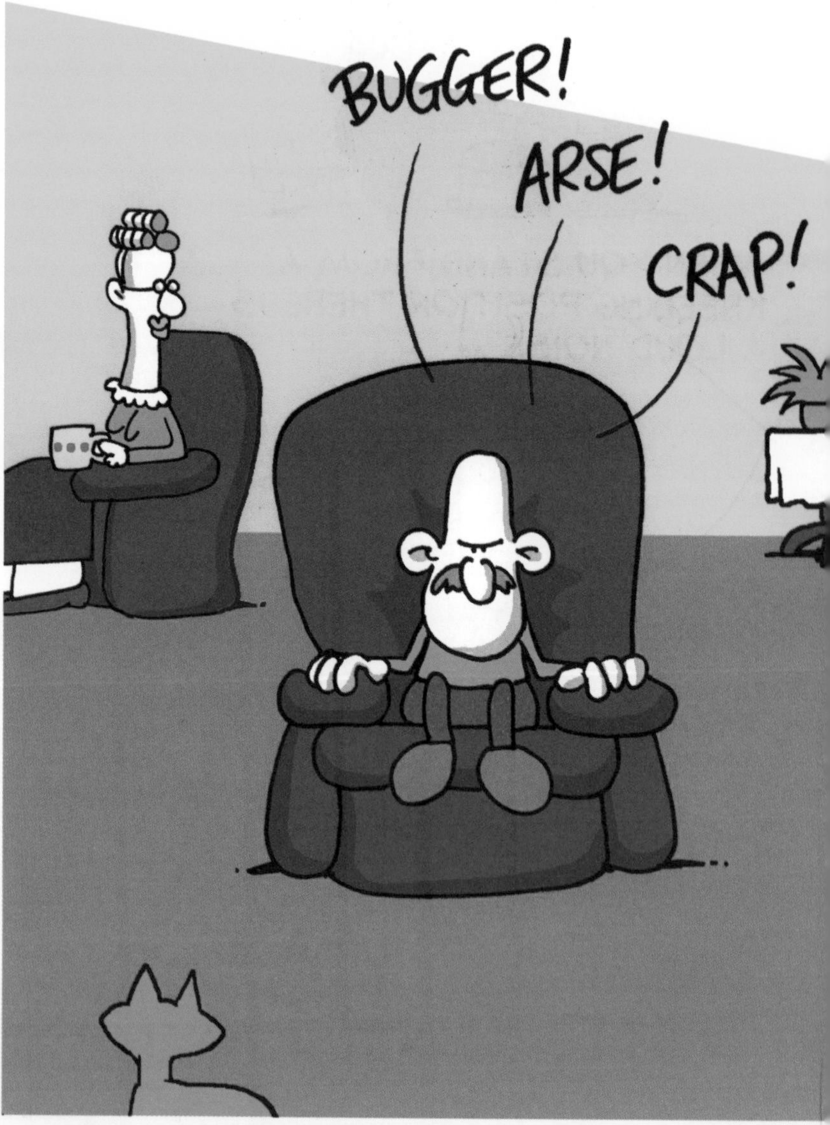
BUGGER!
ARSE!
CRAP!

MAUDE FINALLY COMES TO REALISE THAT OVER TIME HER BUM HAD MOVED SOUTH

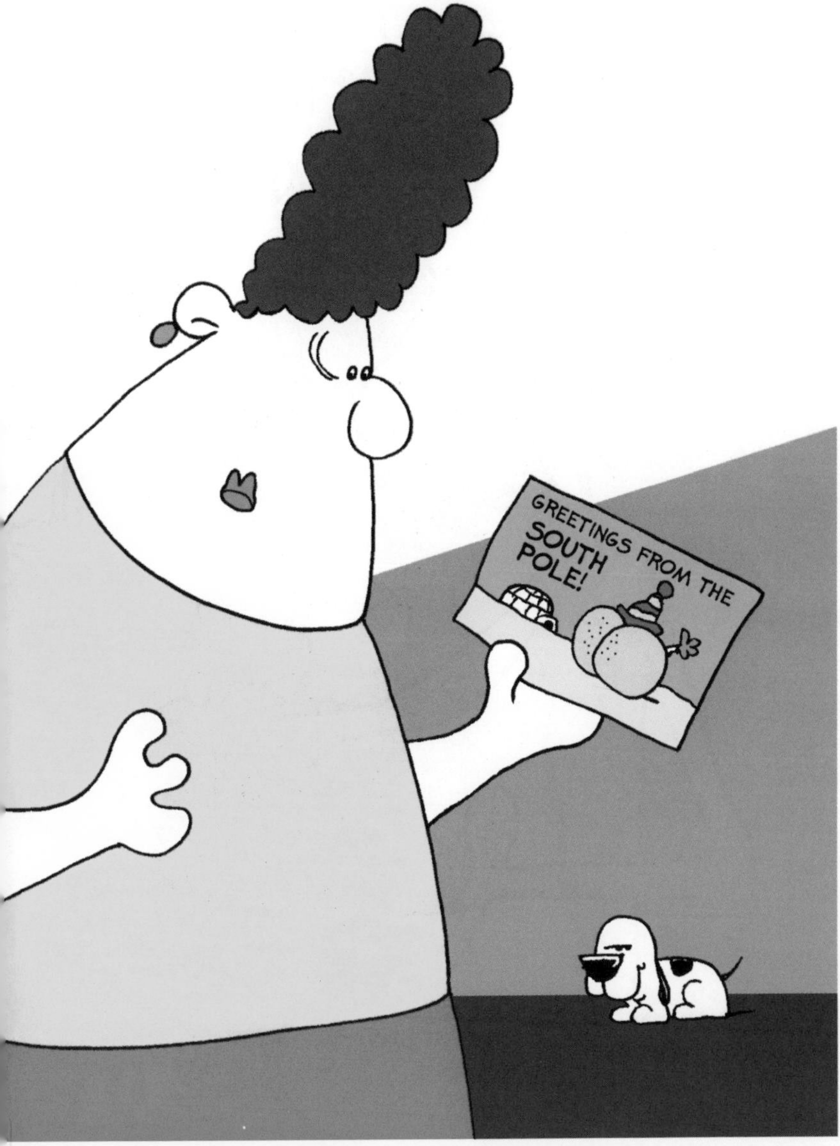
GREETINGS FROM THE
SOUTH
POLE!

JEFF HAD NO NEED FOR WOMEN EVER SINCE HE HAD DEVELOPED HIS VERY OWN SET OF 'BEER BOOBS!'

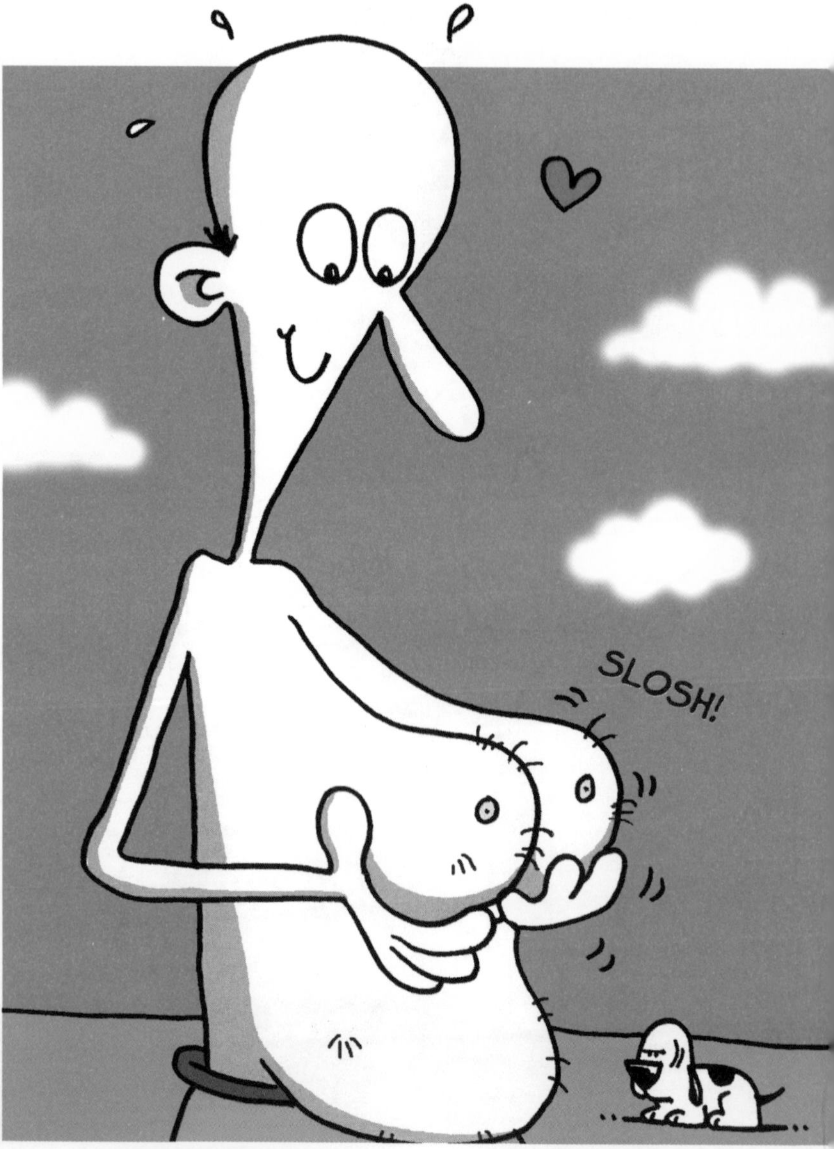
SLOSH!

IN HER RETIREMENT, LILY LIKED TO MAKE BALLOON ANIMALS AT CHILDREN'S PARTIES, ONLY SHE DIDN'T USE BALLOONS

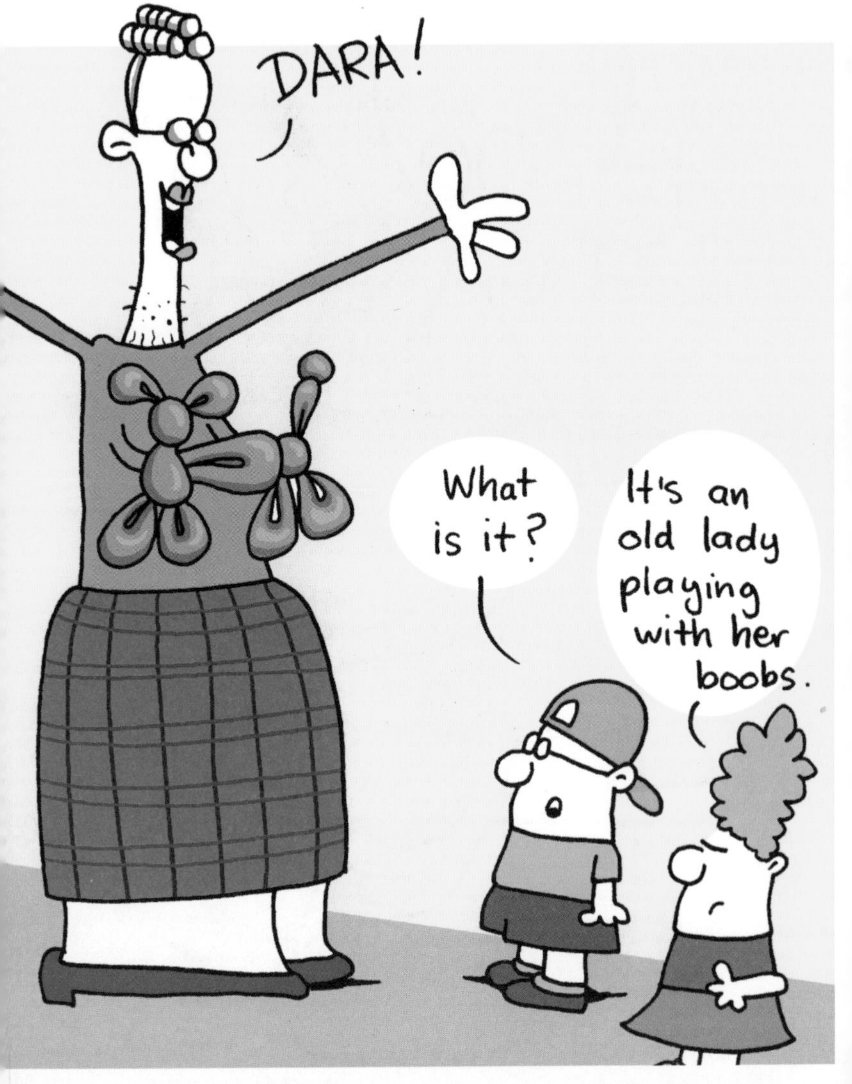
DARA!
What is it?
It's an old lady playing with her boobs.

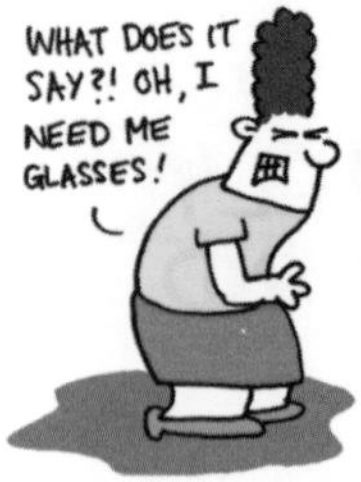
WHAT DOES IT SAY?! OH, I NEED ME GLASSES!

HOW TO PREPARE FOR Getting Old!

1. PRACTISE YOUR CHEEK PINCHING TECHNIQUE! (THE HARDER THE BETTER!)

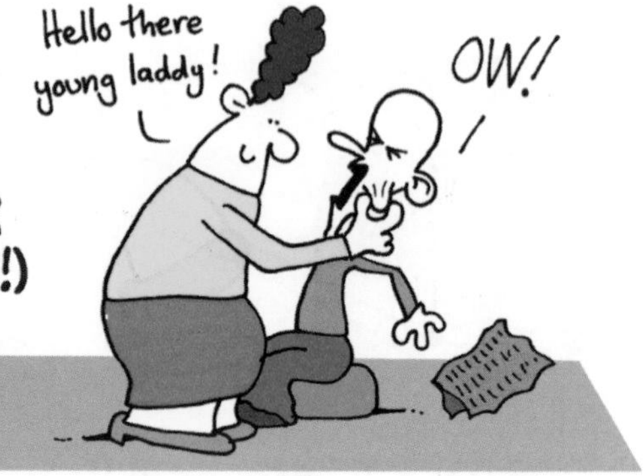
Hello there young laddy!
OW!

2. TRY TO TELL RAMBLING STORIES WITH ABSOLUTELY NO POINT OR COMEDY.

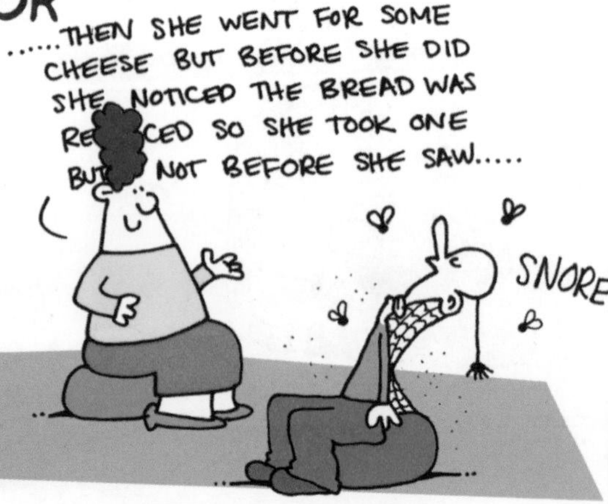
......THEN SHE WENT FOR SOME CHEESE BUT BEFORE SHE DID SHE NOTICED THE BREAD WAS RE CED SO SHE TOOK ONE BU NOT BEFORE SHE SAW.....
SNORE

3. TAKE FAR TOO LONG AT CHECKOUTS BY CONTINUALLY DROPPING YOUR CHANGE AND APOLOGISING!

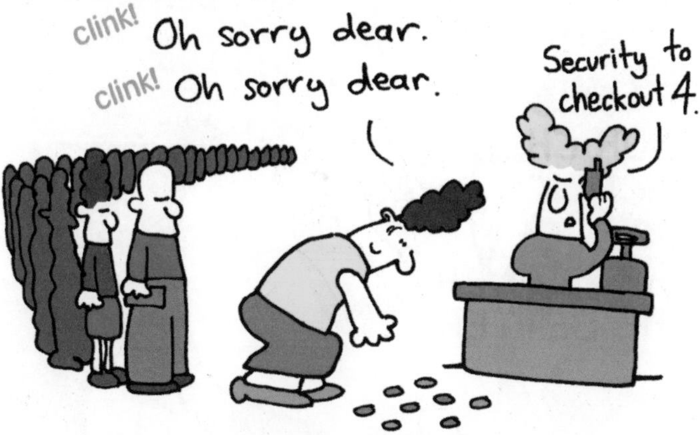
clink!
Oh sorry dear.
clink!
Oh sorry dear.
Security to checkout 4.

4. SURROUND YOURSELF IN THE CORRECT SMELL BY SOAKING YOUR CLOTHES IN WEE!

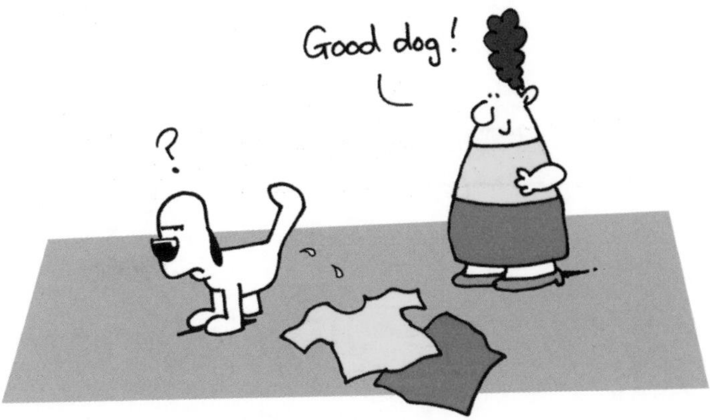
Good dog!
?

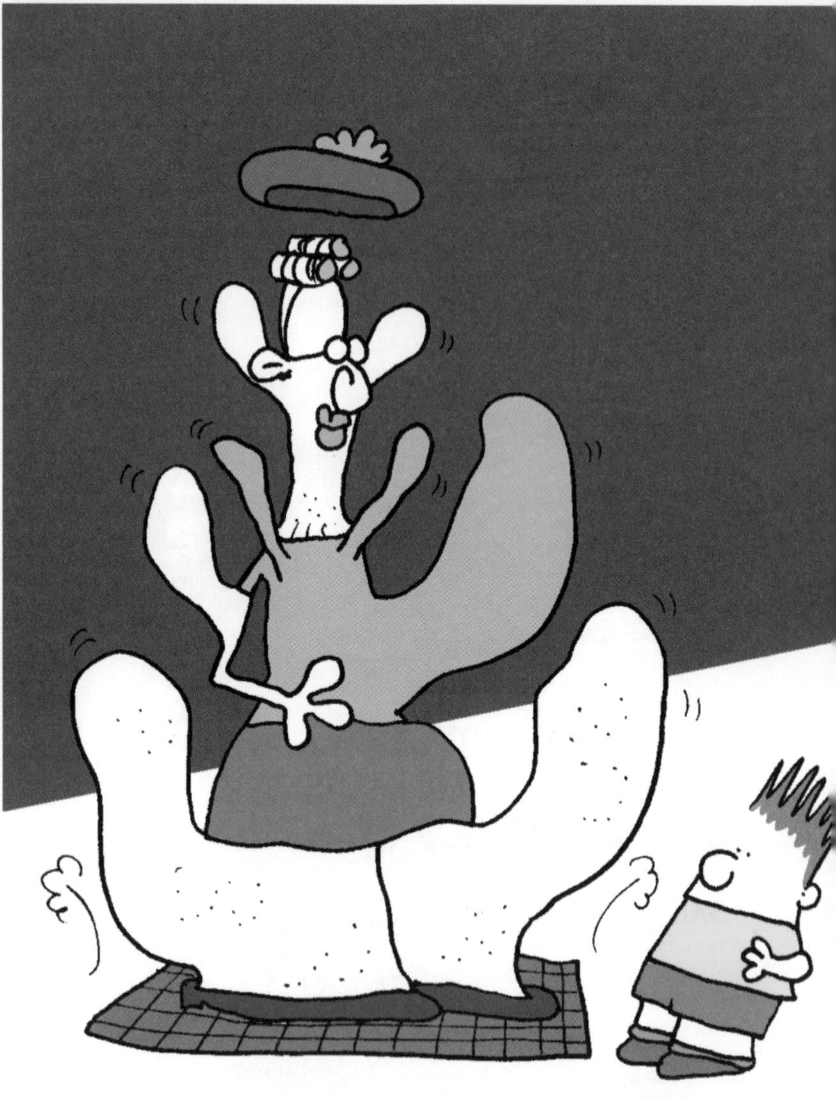

LILY MAKES THE MISTAKE OF ACCIDENTALLY WALKING OVER AN AIR VENT

SOME USES FOR A MAN'S HUGE OLD PANTS!

1. A MARQUEE FOR BEER FESTIVALS AND WEDDINGS!

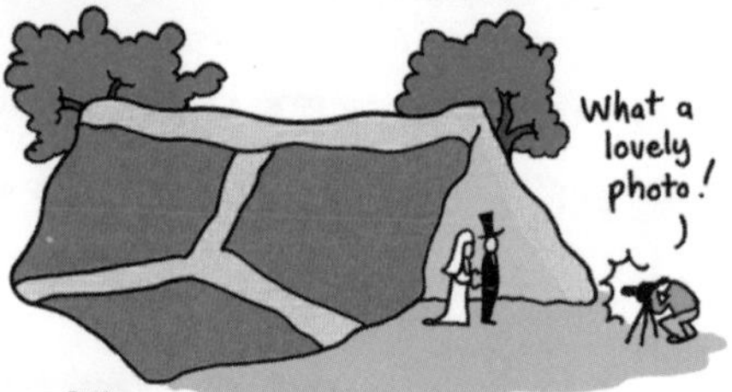
What a lovely photo!

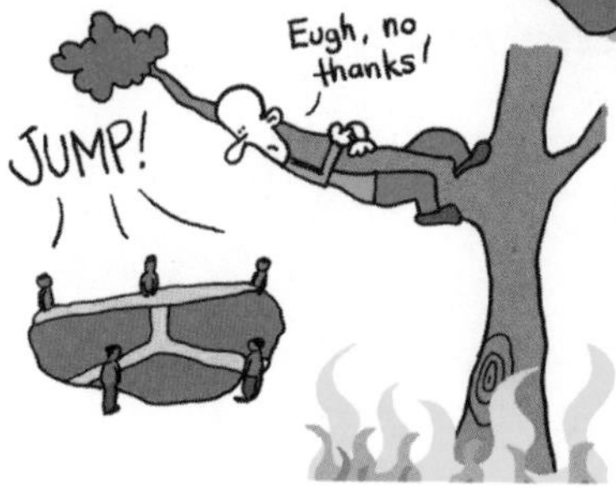
Eugh, no thanks!
JUMP!

2. A SAFETY NET FOR CIRCUS ACTS OR FIRE RESCUES!

3. A CHAMPIONSHIP YACHT SAIL!

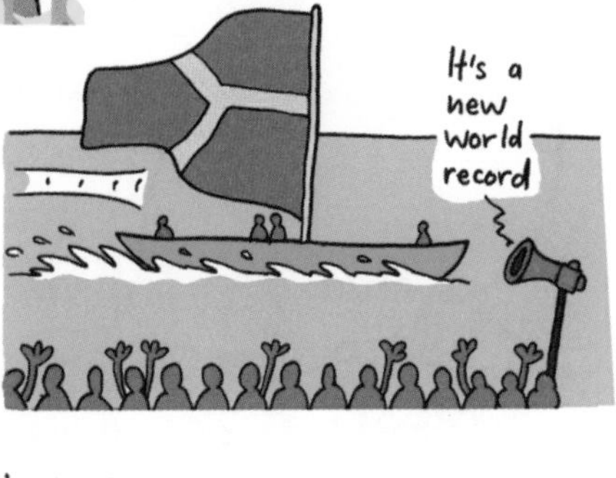
It's a new world record

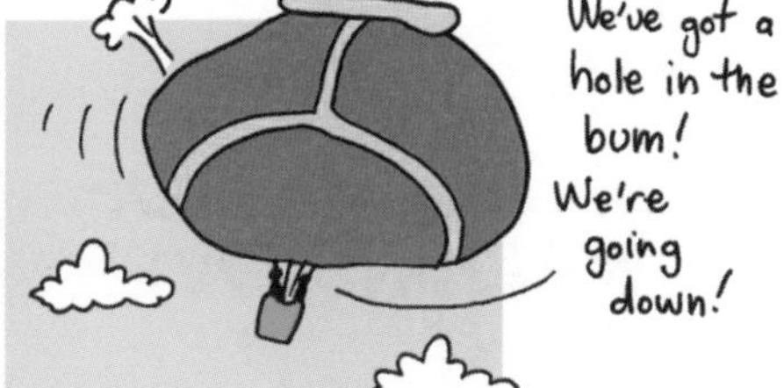
PSSSSSSSS!
We've got a hole in the bum!
We're going down!

4. AN AIR BALLOON FOR AROUND THE WORLD FLIGHTS!

HOW TO PRETEND YOU'RE YOUNGER THAN YOU ARE!

1. CULTIVATE TEENAGE ZITS BY EATING TONS OF CHOCCIES AND DIPPING YOUR FACE IN GREASE!

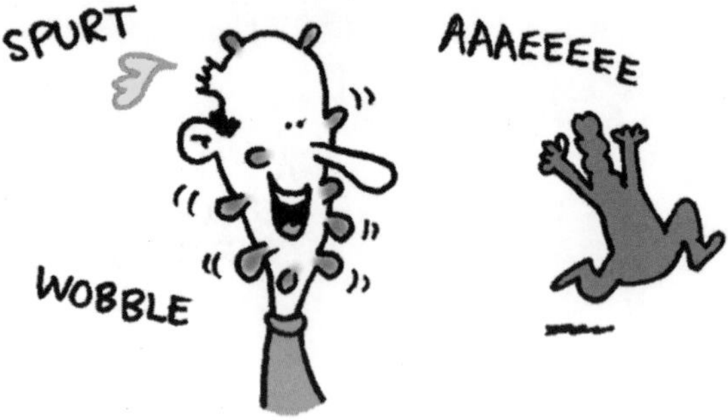
SPURT
AAAEEEEEE
WOBBLE

2. PLAY LOUD MUSIC IN YOUR ROOM!

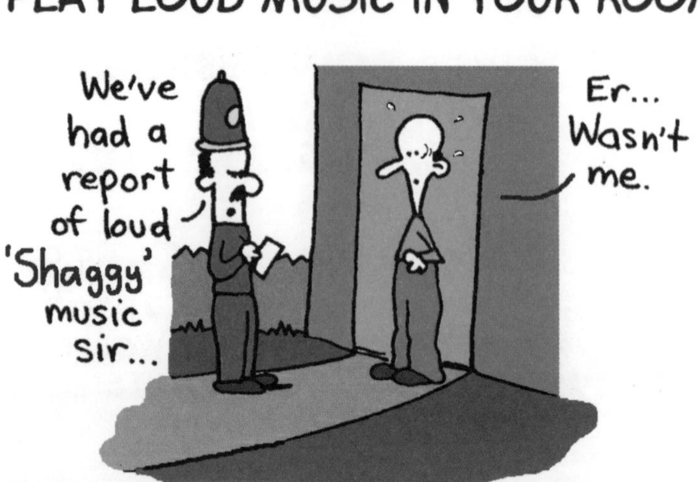
We've had a report of loud 'Shaggy' music sir...
Er... Wasn't me.

3. DON'T CHANGE YOUR UNDERWEAR FOR DAYS!

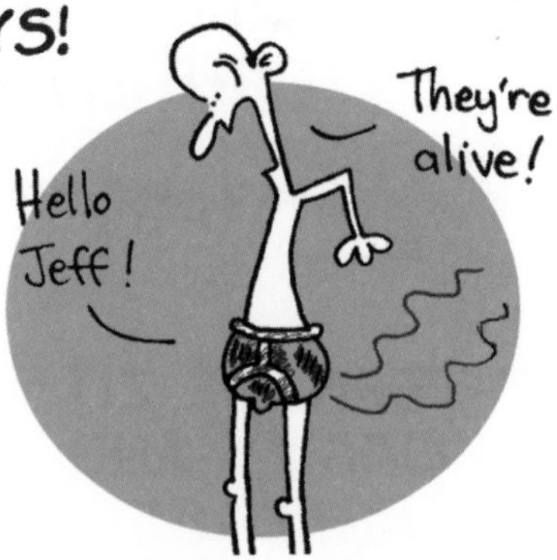
They're alive!
Hello Jeff!

4. ACT IMMATURE BY BLOWING OFF IN PEOPLE'S FACES!

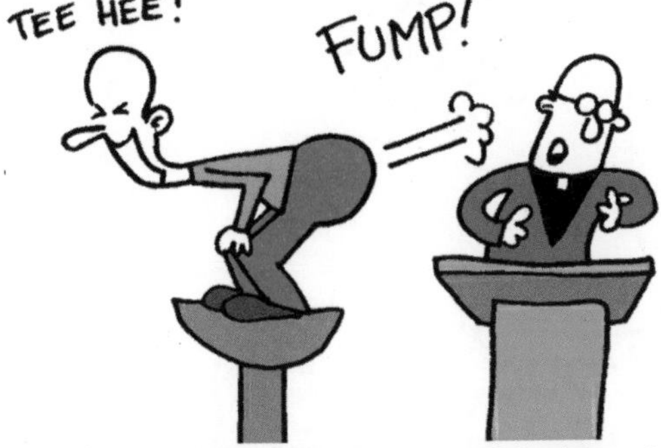
TEE HEE!
FUMP!

5. GET PIERCED SOMEWHERE UNUSUAL!

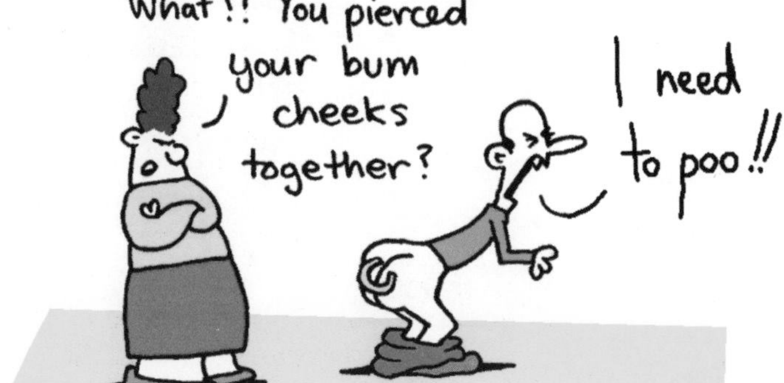
What?! You pierced your bum cheeks together?
I need to poo!!

LILY COULDN'T HELP BE SLIGHTLY OFFENDED BY ALF'S BIRTHDAY GIFT

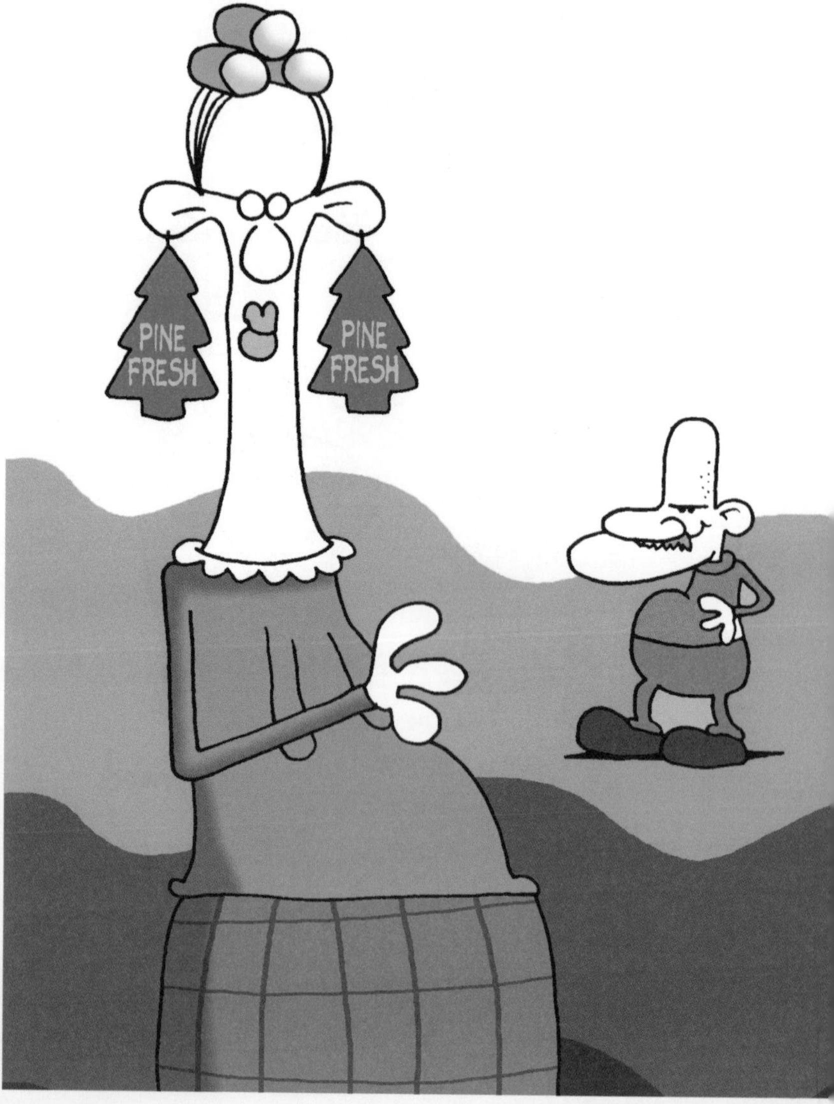
PINE FRESH
PINE FRESH

DURING DINNER, LILY REALISED SHE HAD SOMETHING CAUGHT IN HER TEETH

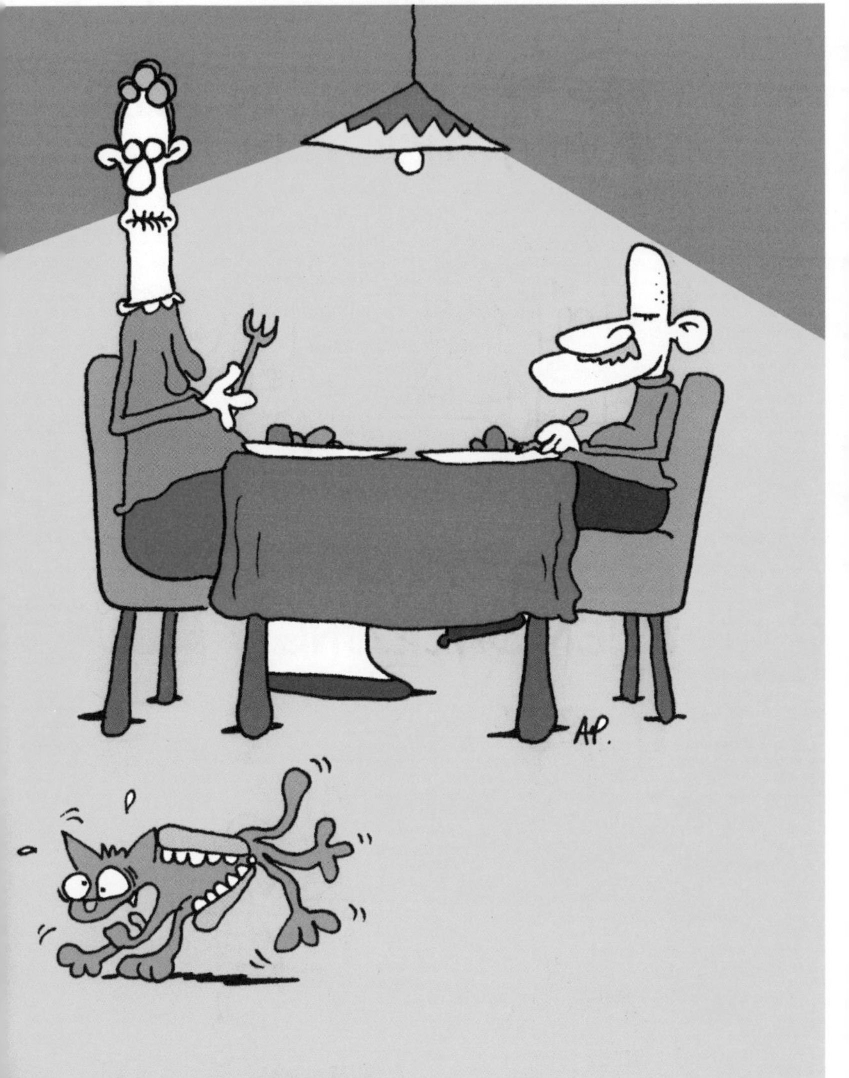
AP.

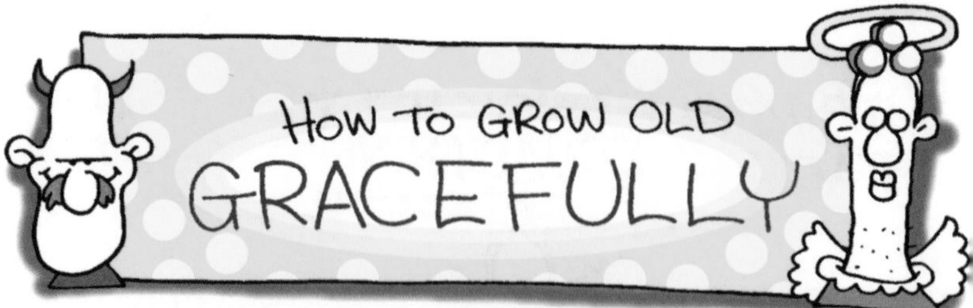
HOW TO GROW OLD
GRACEFULLY

1. KEEP THE LABEL IN YOUR TOUPEE TUCKED IN

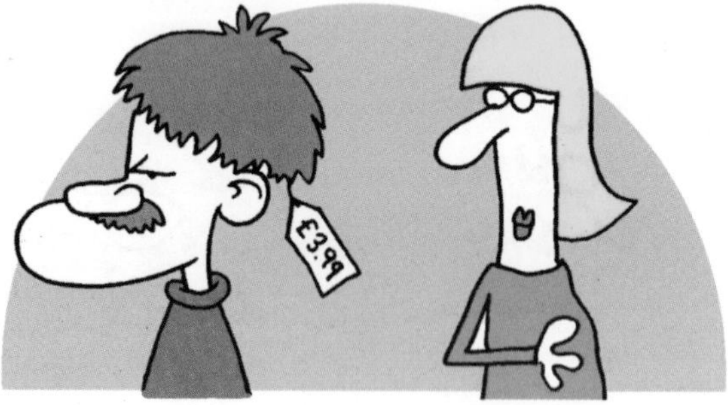
£3.99

2. COVER YOUR MOUTH WHEN SNEEZING

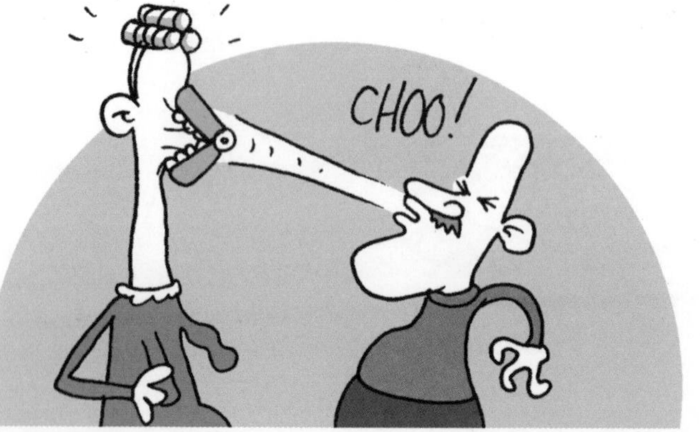
CHOO!

3. TRIM ALL UNSIGHTLY FACIAL HAIR

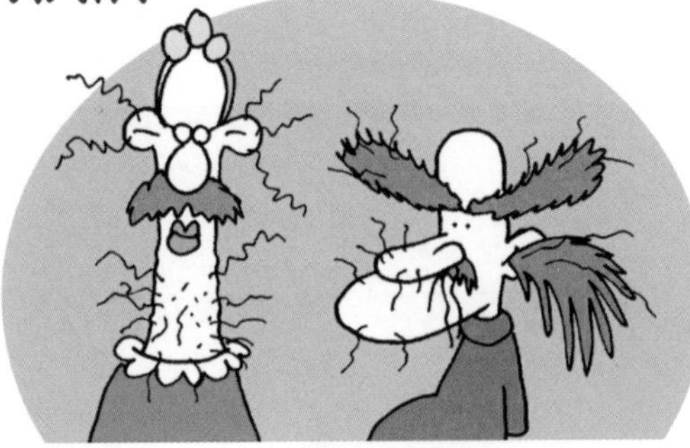

4. TAPE UP SECTIONS WHICH ARE SAGGING NOTICEABLY

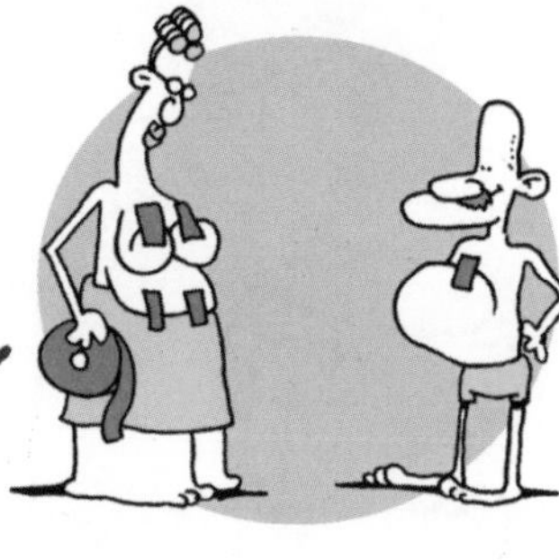

5. KEEP A PUNCTURE REPAIR KIT HANDY FOR INCONTINENCE PANT LEAKS!

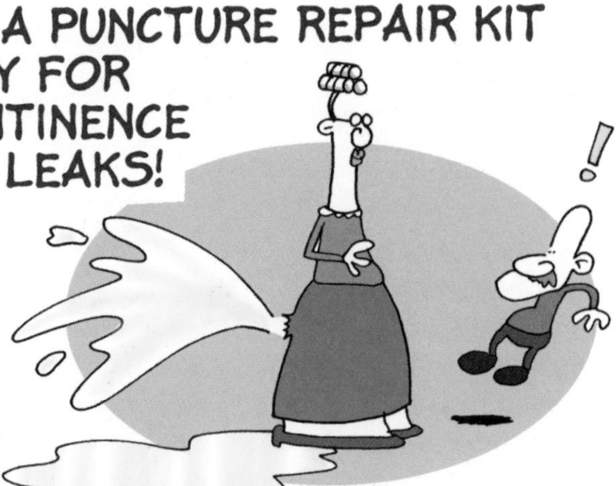

ONCE AGAIN, ALF SPENT THE NIGHT "ON THE PISS"

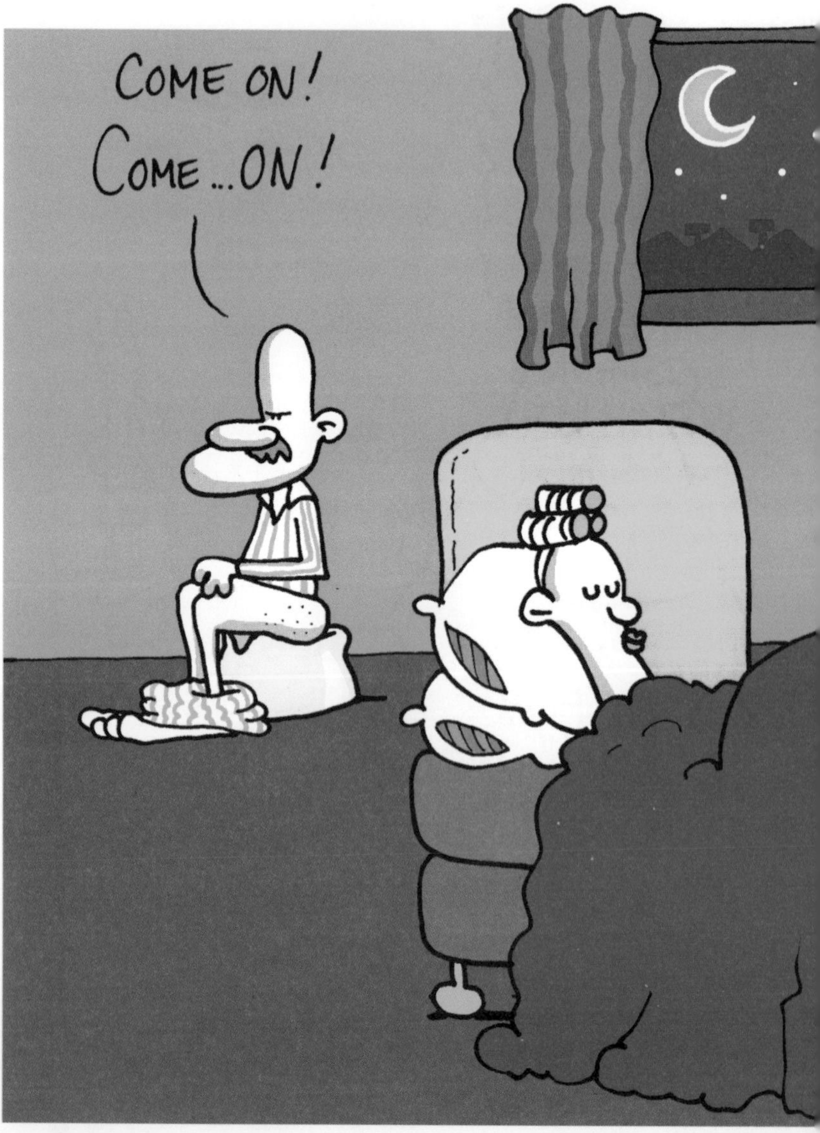
COME ON!
COME...ON!

DURING THE SUMMER, MAUDE LIKES TO WEAR BOOB TUBES

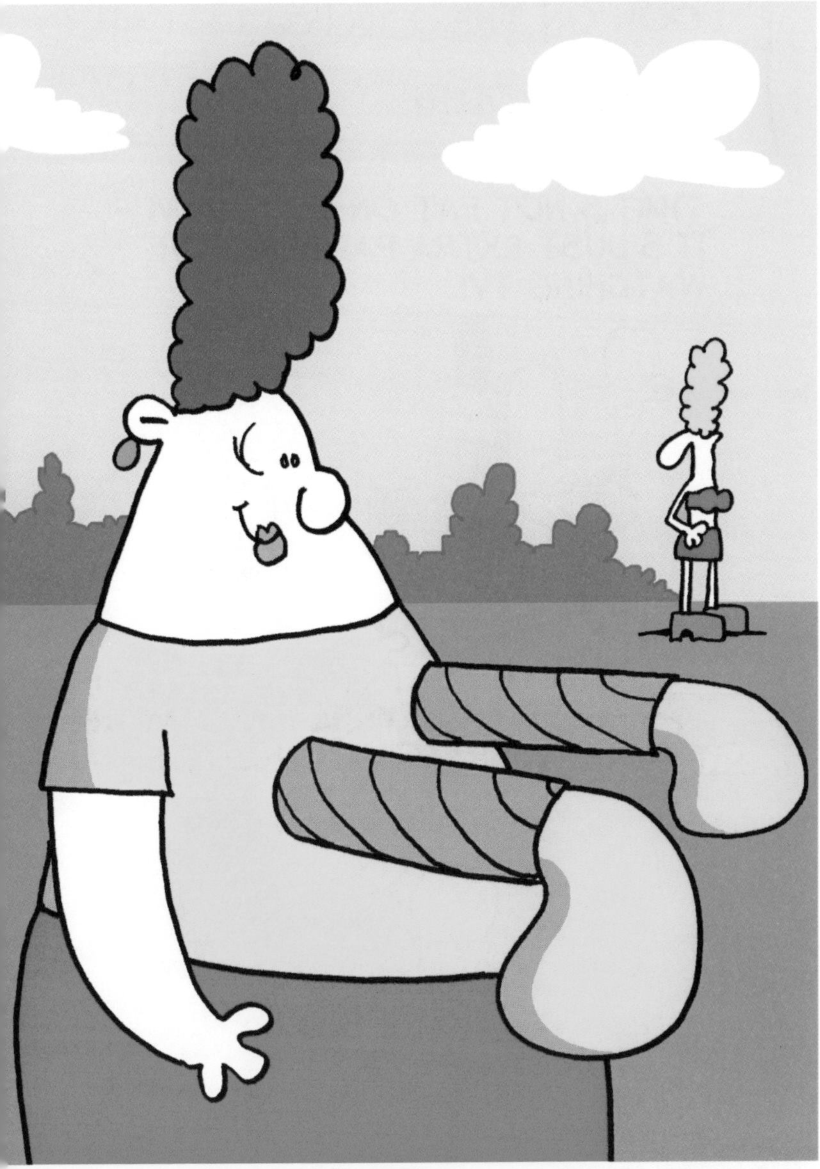

LOOK ON THE BRIGHT SIDE NOW YOU'RE OLDER!

1. THAT'S NOT FAT ON YOUR BUM – IT'S JUST EXTRA PADDING FOR WATCHING TV!

2. EYESIGHT FAILING? YOUR FRIENDS WILL LOOK MORE ATTRACTIVE IN SOFT FOCUS!

3. CAN'T HANDLE YOUR DRINK LIKE YOU USED TO? THINK OF THE MONEY YOU'LL SAVE!

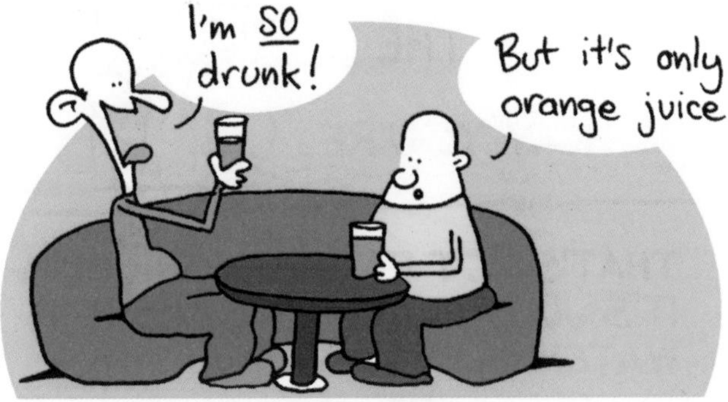

I'm SO drunk!
But it's only orange juice

BOWEL MOVEMENTS: JUST BE GRATEFUL YOU GET ANY – NO MATTER HOW INFREQUENT!

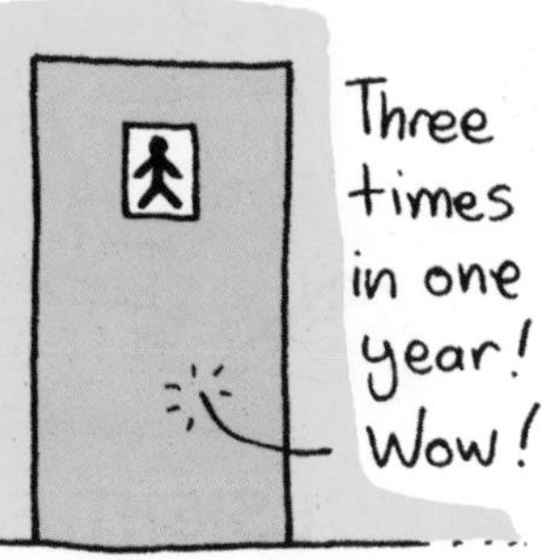

Three times in one year! Wow!

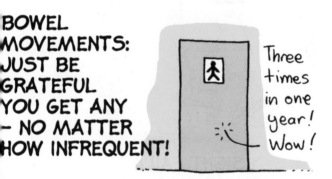

5. SEX: JUST BE GRATEFUL YOU GET ANY – NO MATTER HOW INFREQUENT!

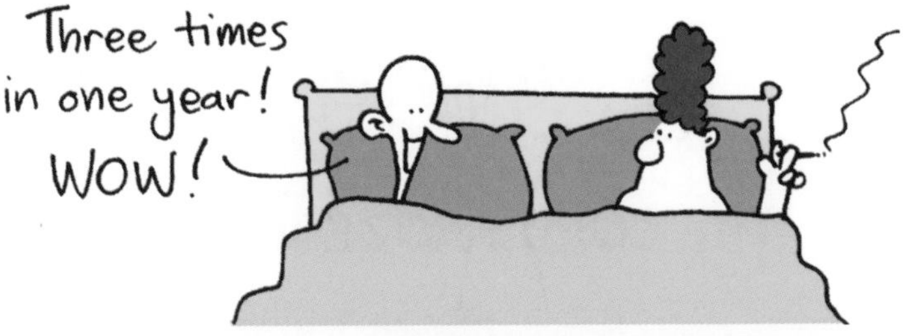

Three times in one year! WOW!

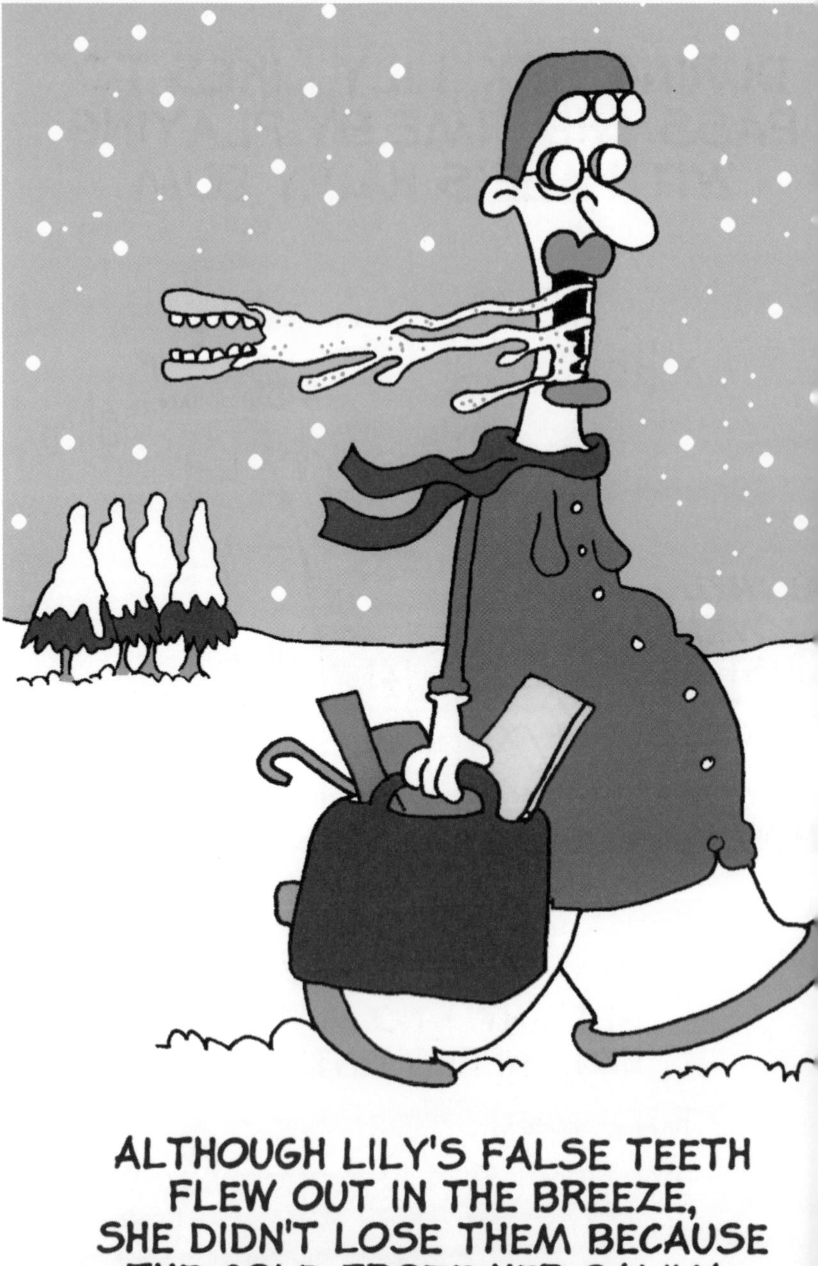

ALTHOUGH LILY'S FALSE TEETH
FLEW OUT IN THE BREEZE,
SHE DIDN'T LOSE THEM BECAUSE
THE COLD FROZE HER SALIVA

DURING SEX, LILY LIKES TO PASS THE TIME BY PLAYING WITH ALF'S HAIRY BUM

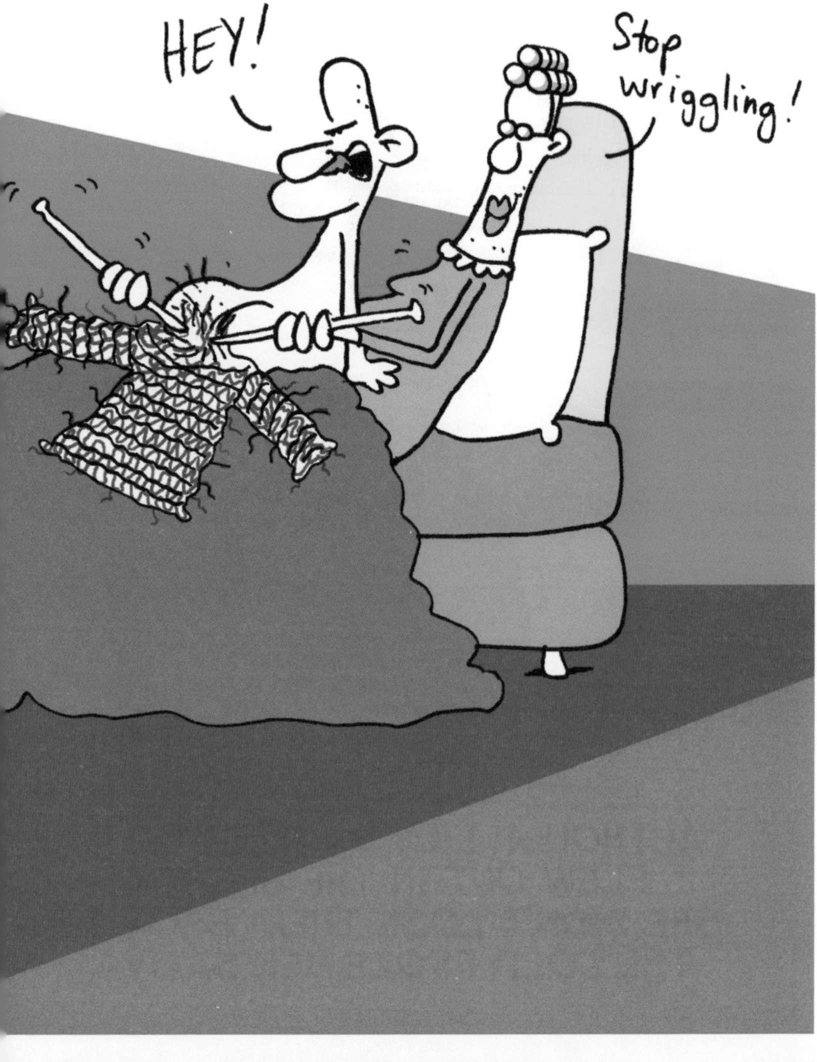
HEY!
Stop wriggling!

ANATOMY OF AN OLD SLAPPER!

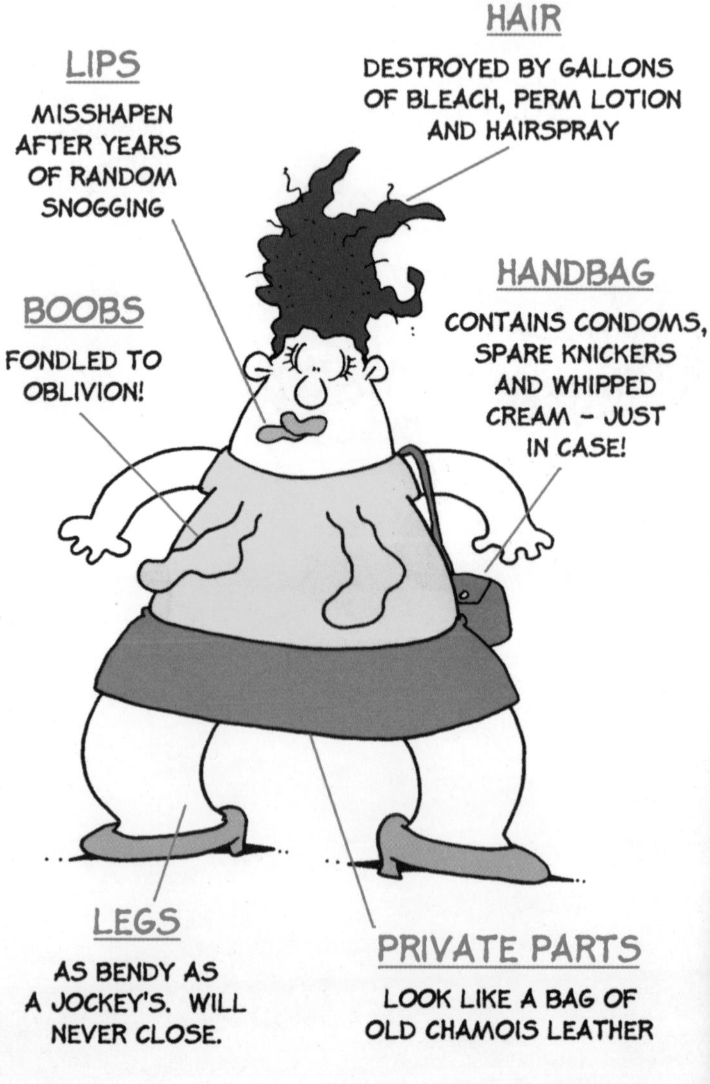

HAIR
DESTROYED BY GALLONS OF BLEACH, PERM LOTION AND HAIRSPRAY
LIPS
MISSHAPEN AFTER YEARS OF RANDOM SNOGGING
HANDBAG
CONTAINS CONDOMS, SPARE KNICKERS AND WHIPPED CREAM – JUST IN CASE!
BOOBS
FONDLED TO OBLIVION!
LEGS
AS BENDY AS A JOCKEY'S. WILL NEVER CLOSE.
PRIVATE PARTS
LOOK LIKE A BAG OF OLD CHAMOIS LEATHER

TOO POOR TO PAY THE HEATING BILLS, LILY AND ALF ARE FORCED TO FIND OTHER WAYS TO KEEP WARM

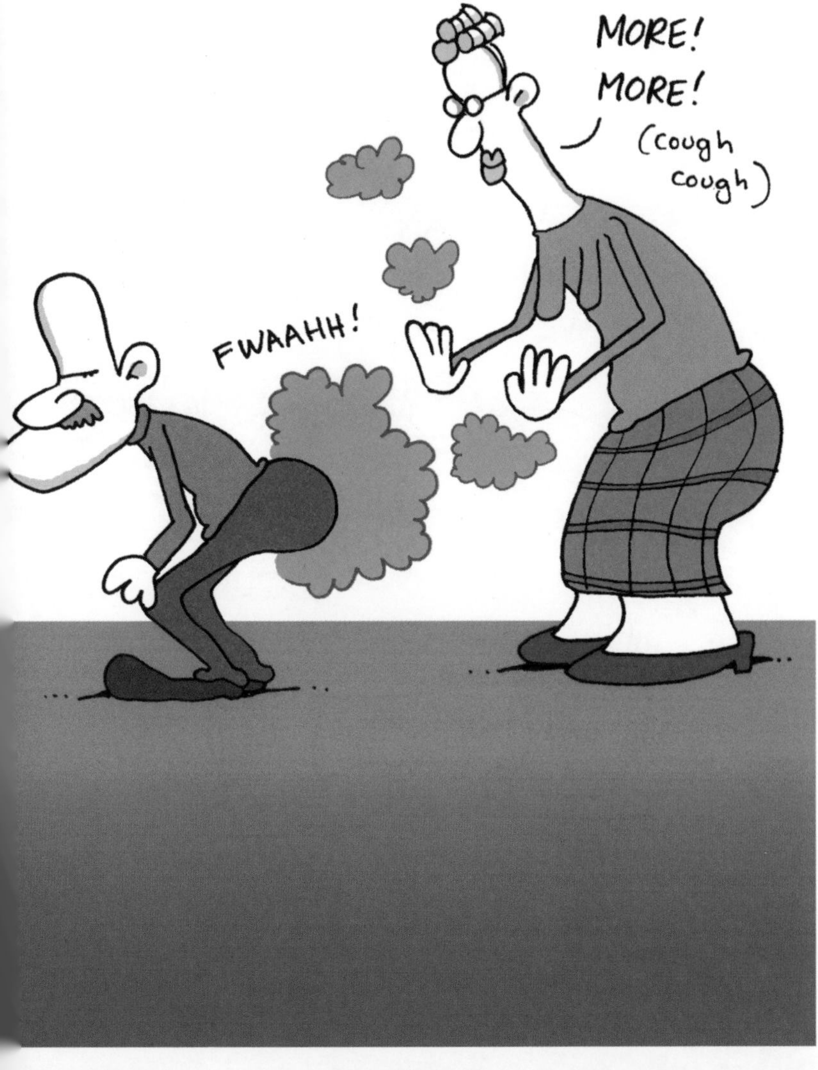

MORE!
MORE!
(cough
cough)
FWAAHH!

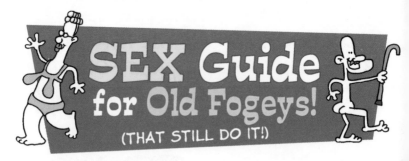

SEX Guide for Old Fogeys!

(THAT STILL DO IT!)

IF YOUR PARTNER STARTS SCREAMING, IT DOESN'T NECESSARILY MEAN THEY'RE HAVING AN ORGASM!

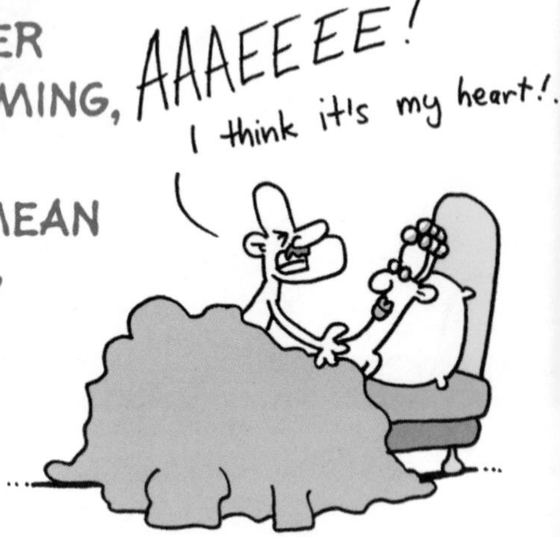
AAAEEEEE!
I think it's my heart!.

COMBINE SEX WITH OLD PEOPLE'S FAVOURITE TV SHOW – COUNTDOWN!

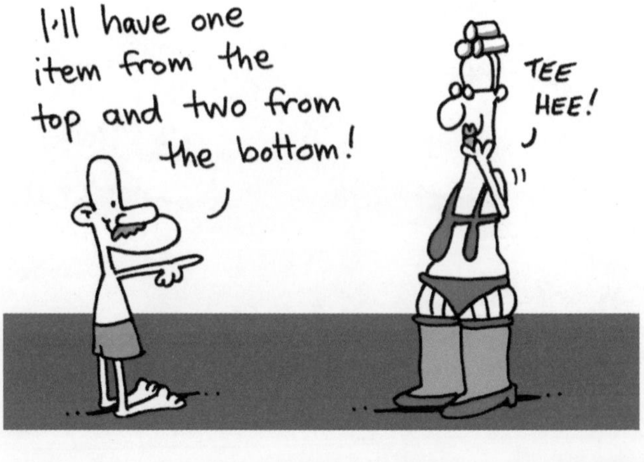
I'll have one item from the top and two from the bottom!
TEE HEE!

WHEN YOU'RE OLDER, IT'S BEST TO AVOID SEX OUTDOORS.

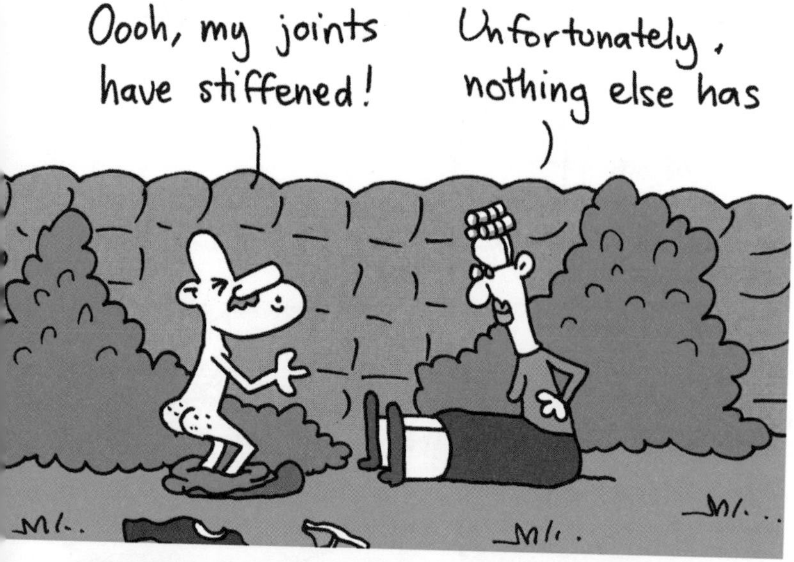
Oooh, my joints have stiffened!
Unfortunately, nothing else has

NEVER BLOW OFF WHILE HE'S 'DOWN THERE' – OLD PERSON'S FARTS CAN KILL!

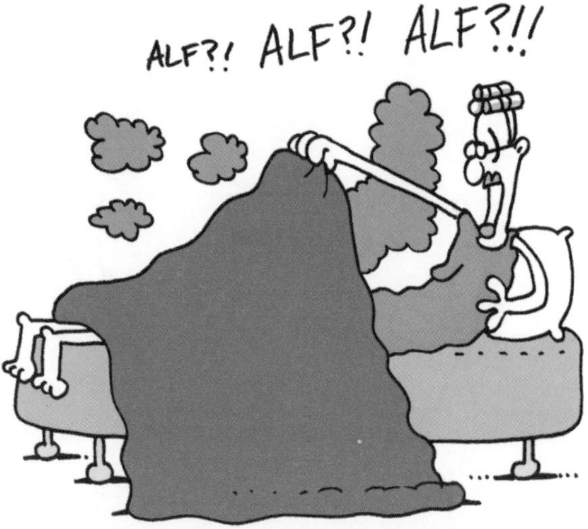
ALF?! ALF?! ALF?!!

WHY OLDER COUPLES SHOULD AVOID TYING EACH OTHER UP DURING LOVE MAKING

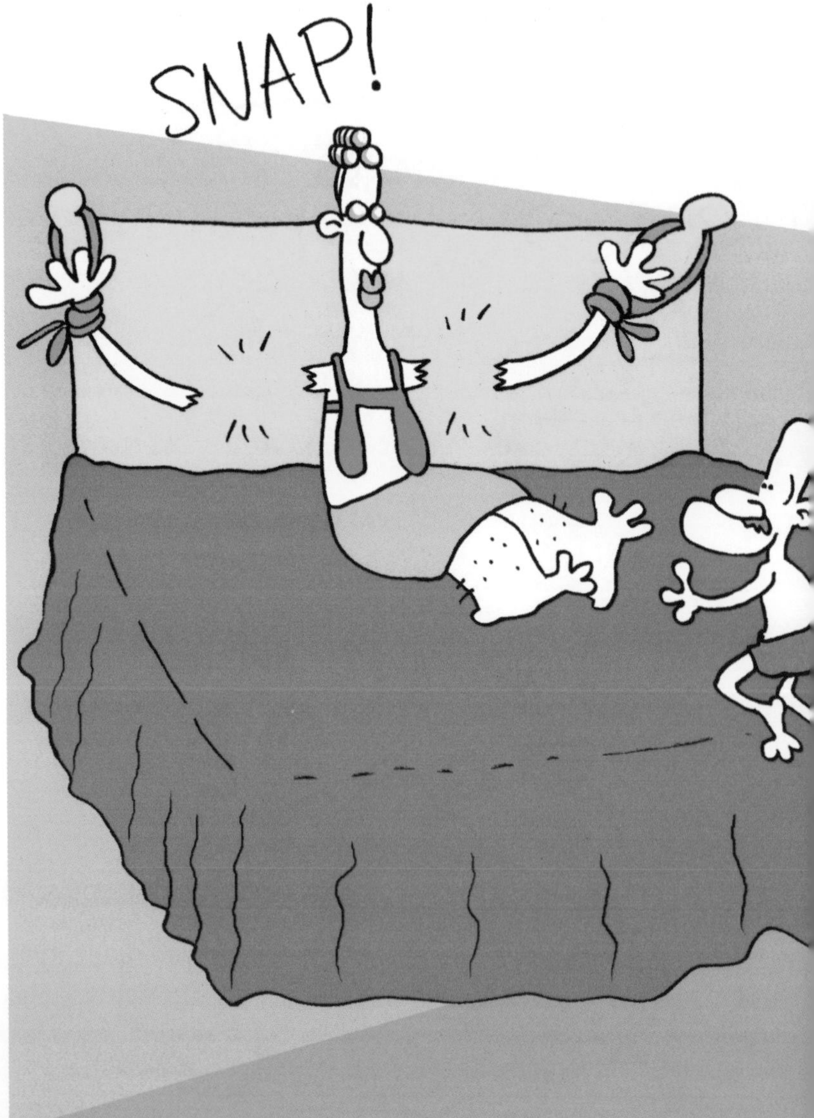
SNAP!

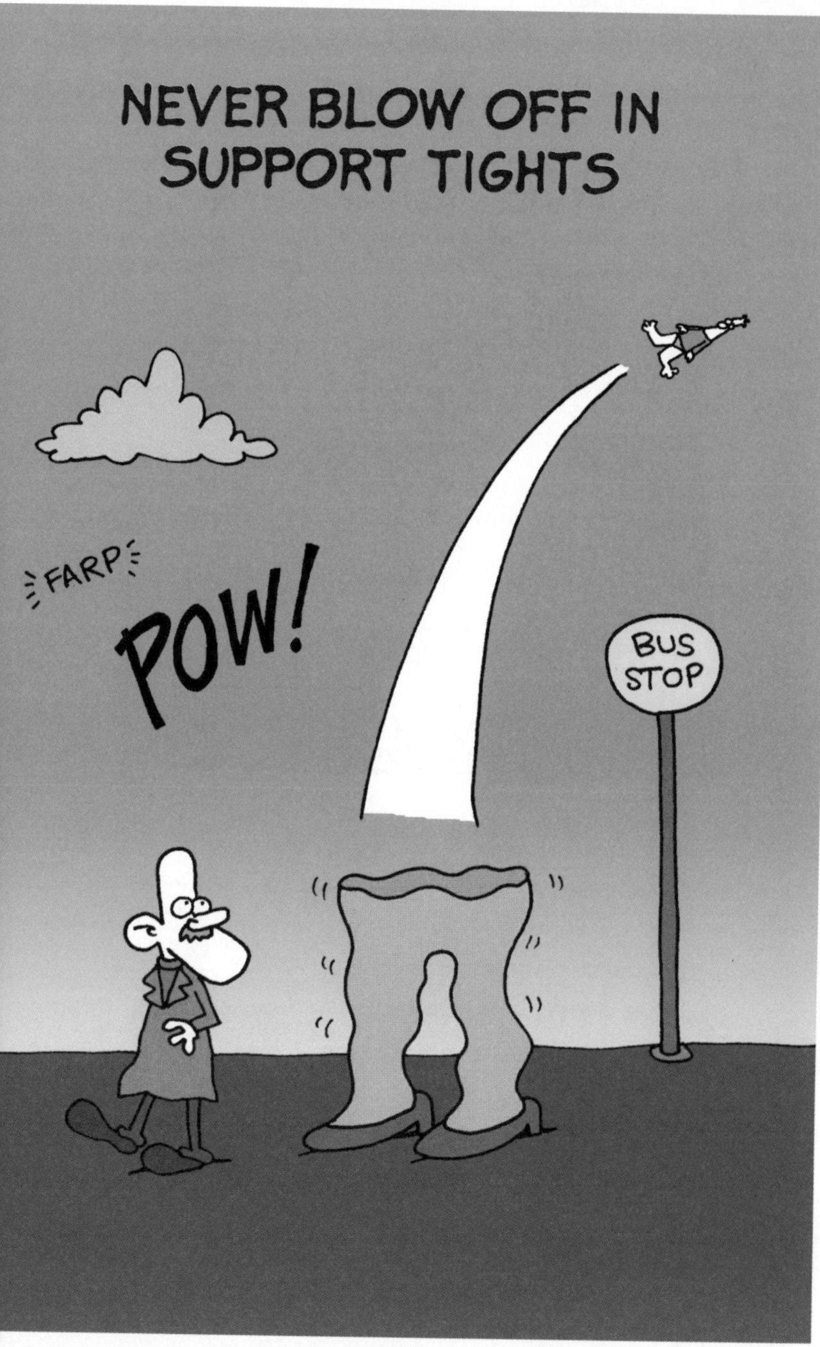
NEVER BLOW OFF IN SUPPORT TIGHTS
FARP
POW!
BUS STOP

HOW TO LIVE TO A RIPE OLD AGE

RULE No 1: NEVER OWN A MOBILE PHONE

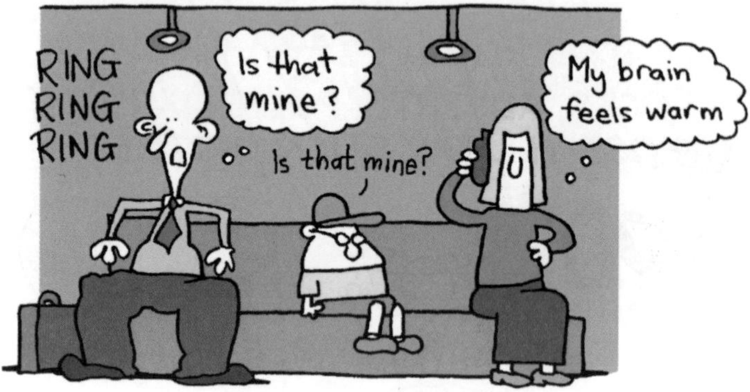
RING
RING
RING
Is that mine?
Is that mine?
My brain feels warm

RULE No 2: NEVER GO ON A DIET

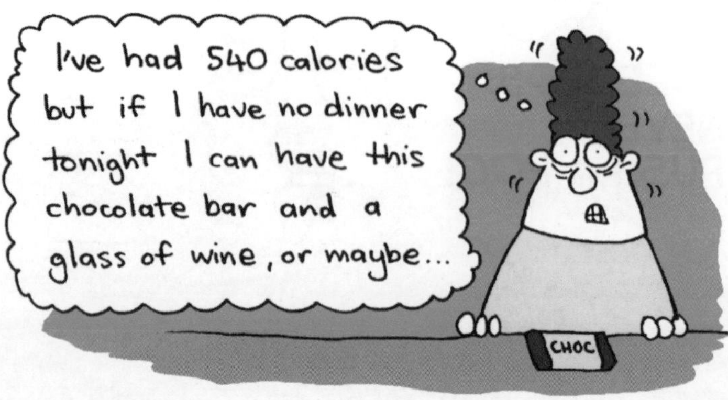
I've had 540 calories but if I have no dinner tonight I can have this chocolate bar and a glass of wine, or maybe...
CHOC

RULE No 3: AVOID ALL FORMS OF TRANSPORT

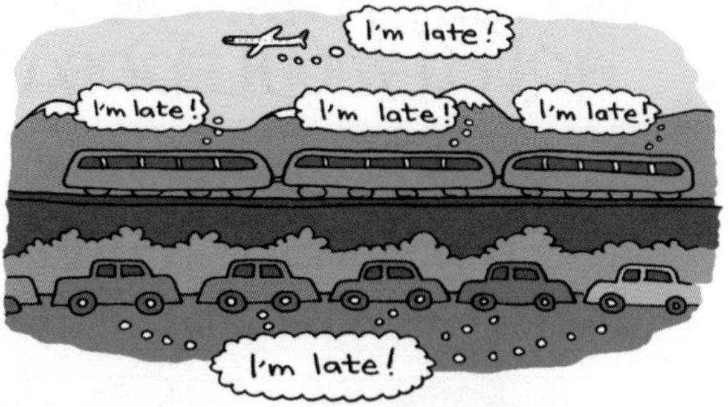
I'm late!
I'm late!
I'm late!
I'm late!
I'm late!

RULE No 4: PAY NO ATTENTION TO CLOCKS, ADVERTS, POLITICIANS OR THOSE YELLOW STICKY NOTES

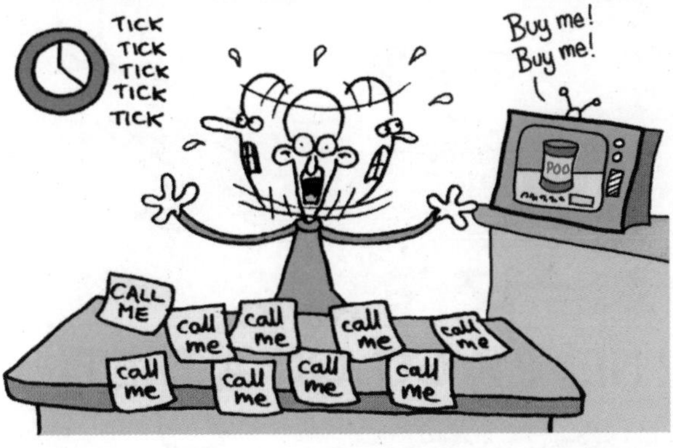
TICK
TICK
TICK
TICK
TICK
Buy me!
Buy me!
POO
CALL ME
call me
call me
call me
call me
call me
call me
call me
call me

RULE No. 5: NEVER RUSH A POO!

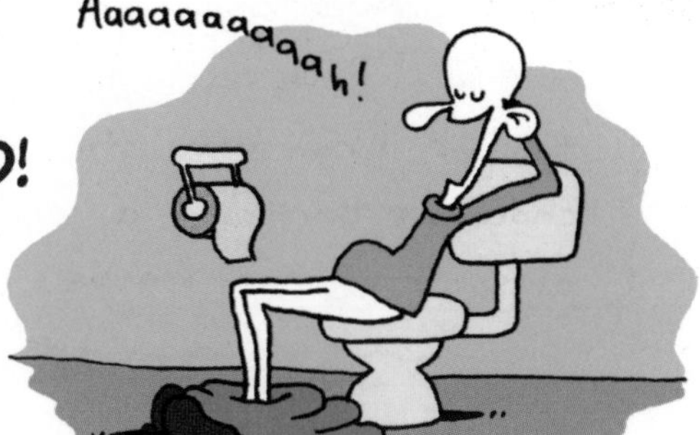
Aaaaaaaaaaah!

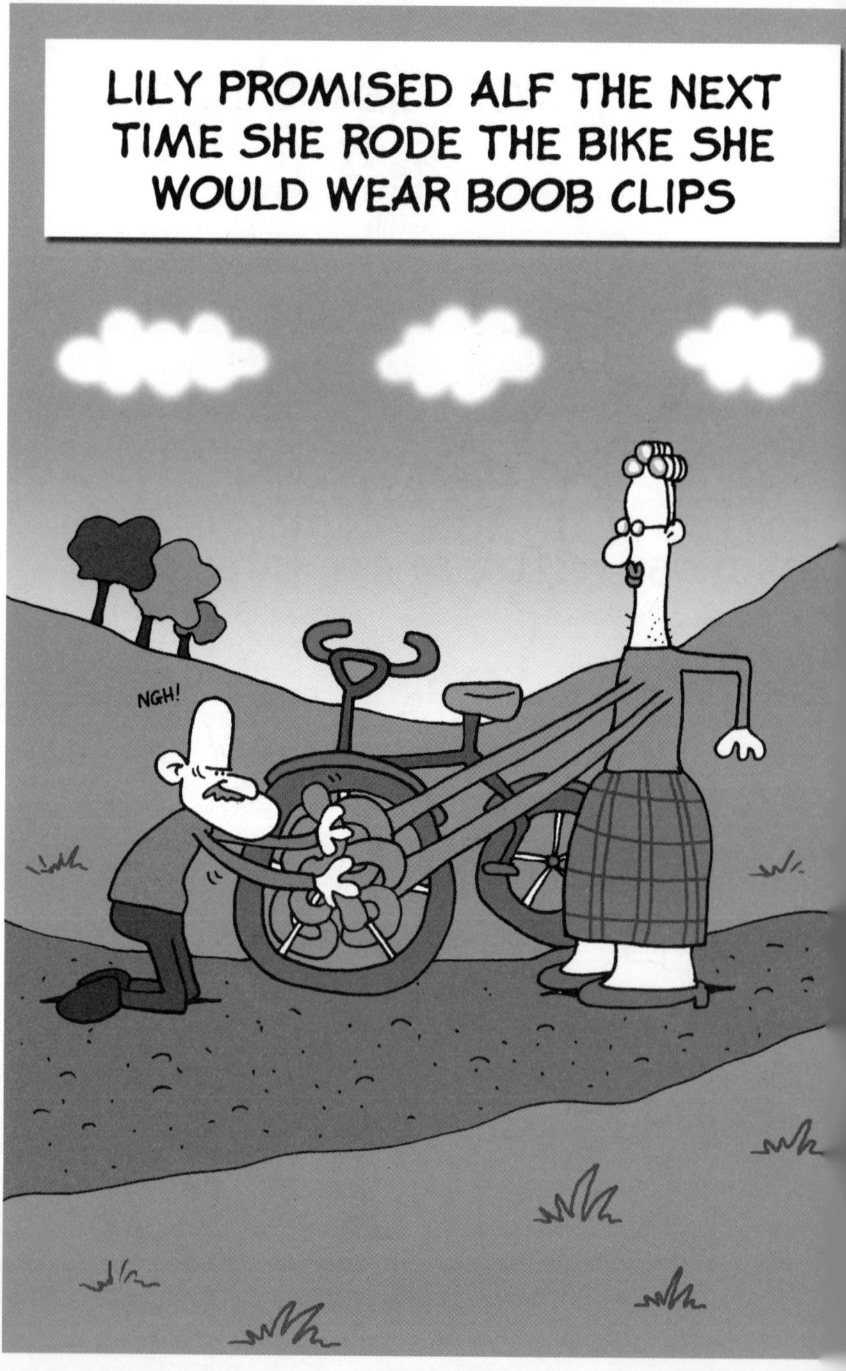
LILY PROMISED ALF THE NEXT TIME SHE RODE THE BIKE SHE WOULD WEAR BOOB CLIPS
NGH!

ALF KNEW TO LEAVE LILY ALONE WHEN SHE WAS GOING THROUGH "THE CHANGE"

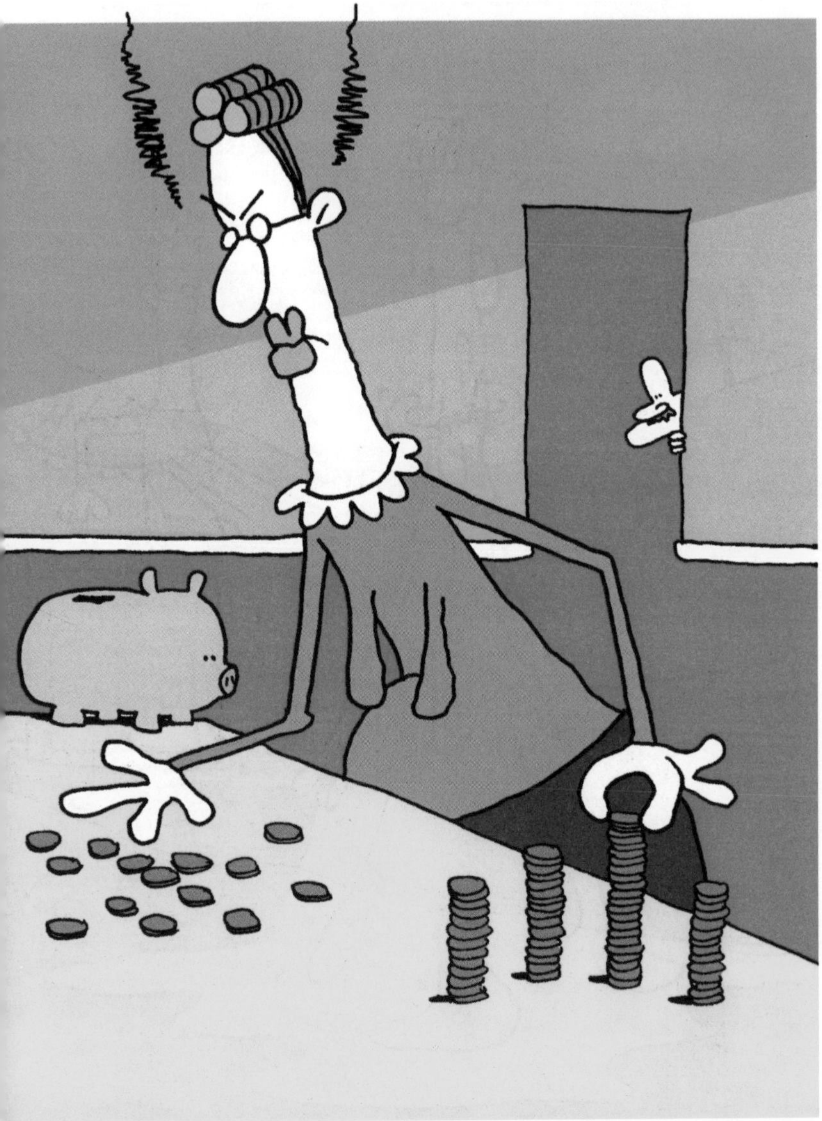

IT HAPPENED ON A TUESDAY AROUND NOON – LILY'S BODY FINALLY GAVE UP ITS BATTLE WITH GRAVITY

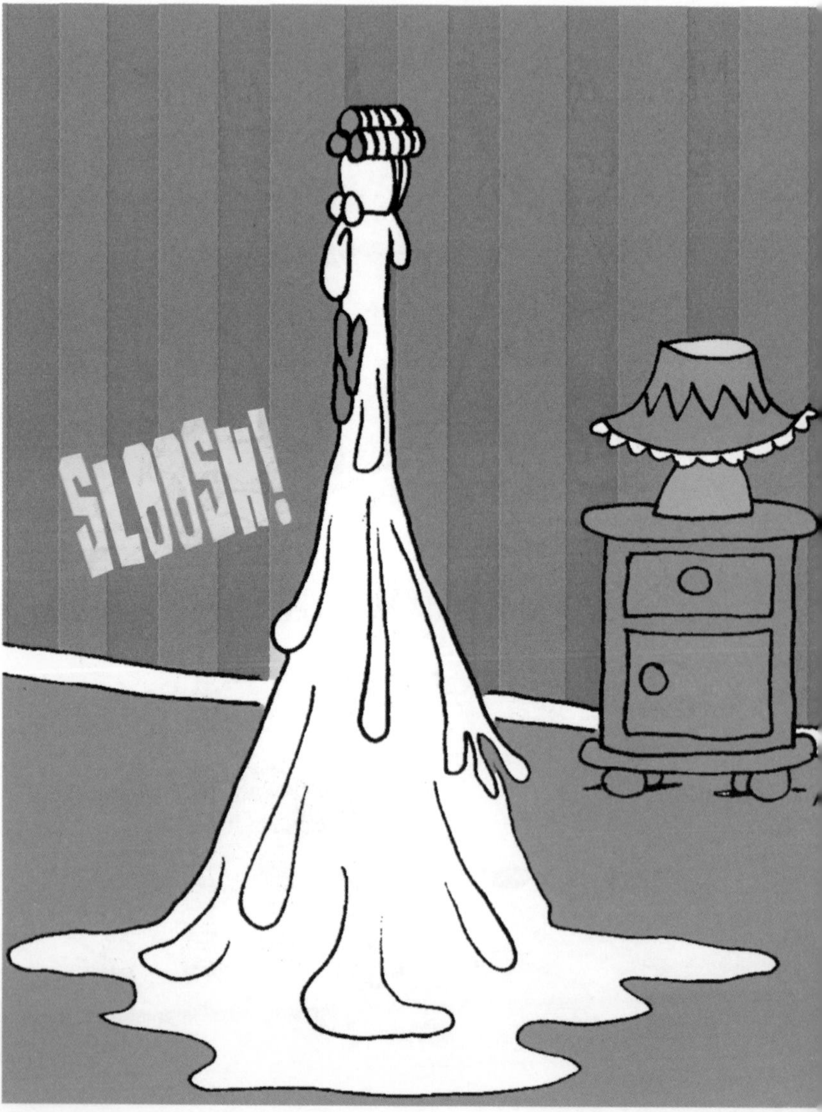
SLOOSH!

AS THEY GROW OLDER, MEN MOVE FROM COMPARING PENIS SIZE TO EAR SIZE

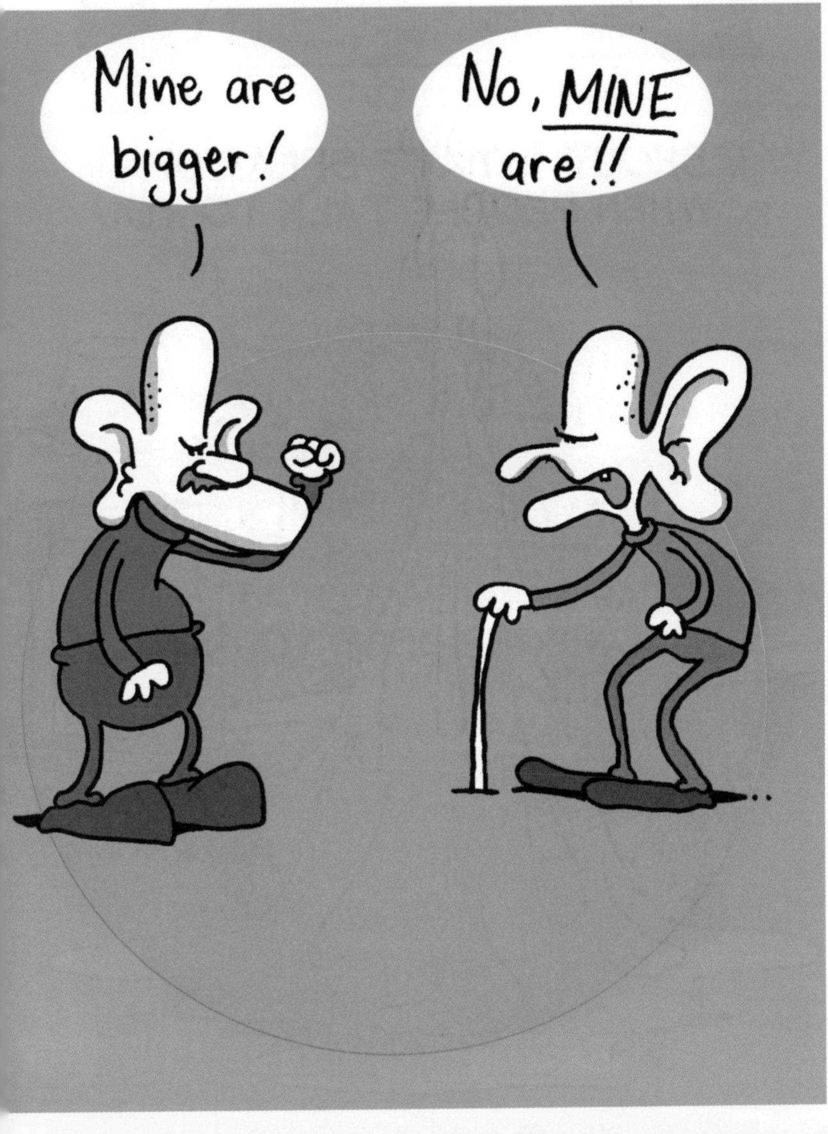
Mine are bigger!
No, MINE are!!

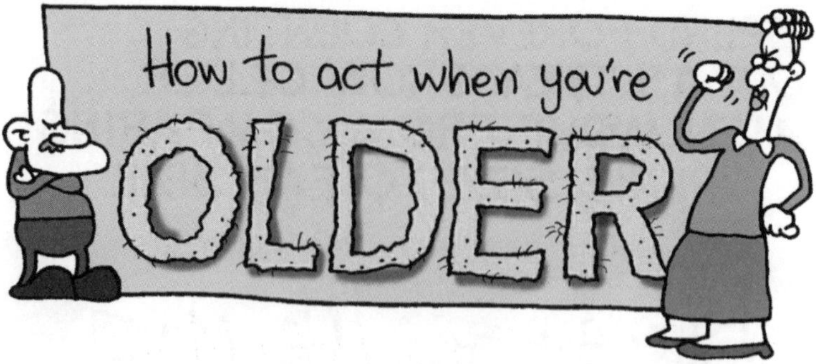
How to act when you're
OLDER

1. SHOUT "WHAT? SPEAK UP!" WHEN PEOPLE TALK TO YOU

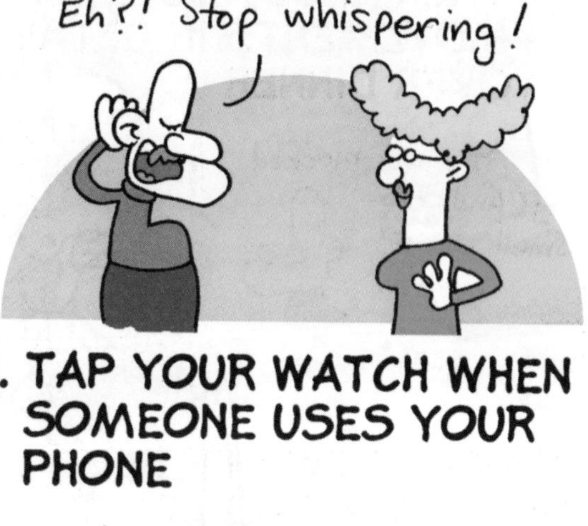
Eh?! Stop whispering!

2. TAP YOUR WATCH WHEN SOMEONE USES YOUR PHONE

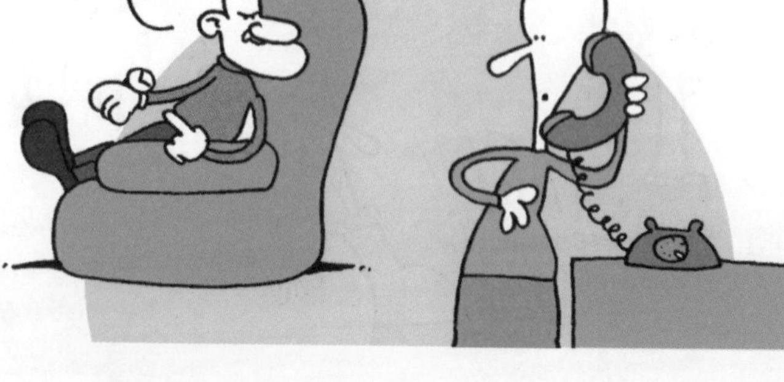
Ahem!

3. SPEND FOREVER COUNTING OUT THE EXACT CHANGE AT TILLS

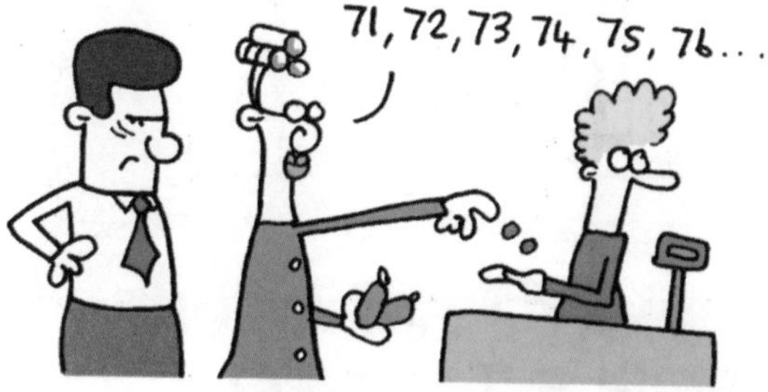
71, 72, 73, 74, 75, 76...

4. TALK ABOUT YOUR BOWEL MOVEMENTS IN DETAIL OVER DINNER

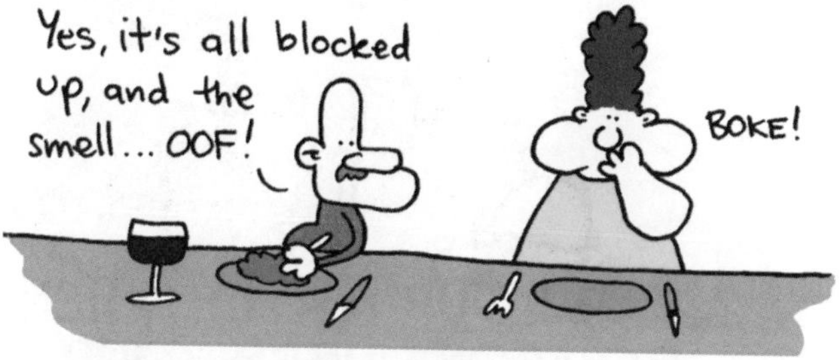
Yes, it's all blocked up, and the smell... OOF!
BOKE!

5. WHEN YOU BLOW OFF IN COMPANY SAY "IT'S MY MEDICATION"

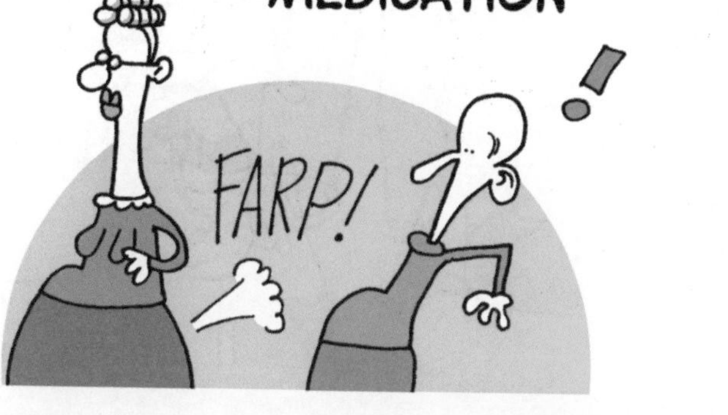
FARP!

SADLY, AS SHE GOT OLDER, LILY LOST THE ABILITY TO CONTROL WHERE AND WHEN SHE PEES

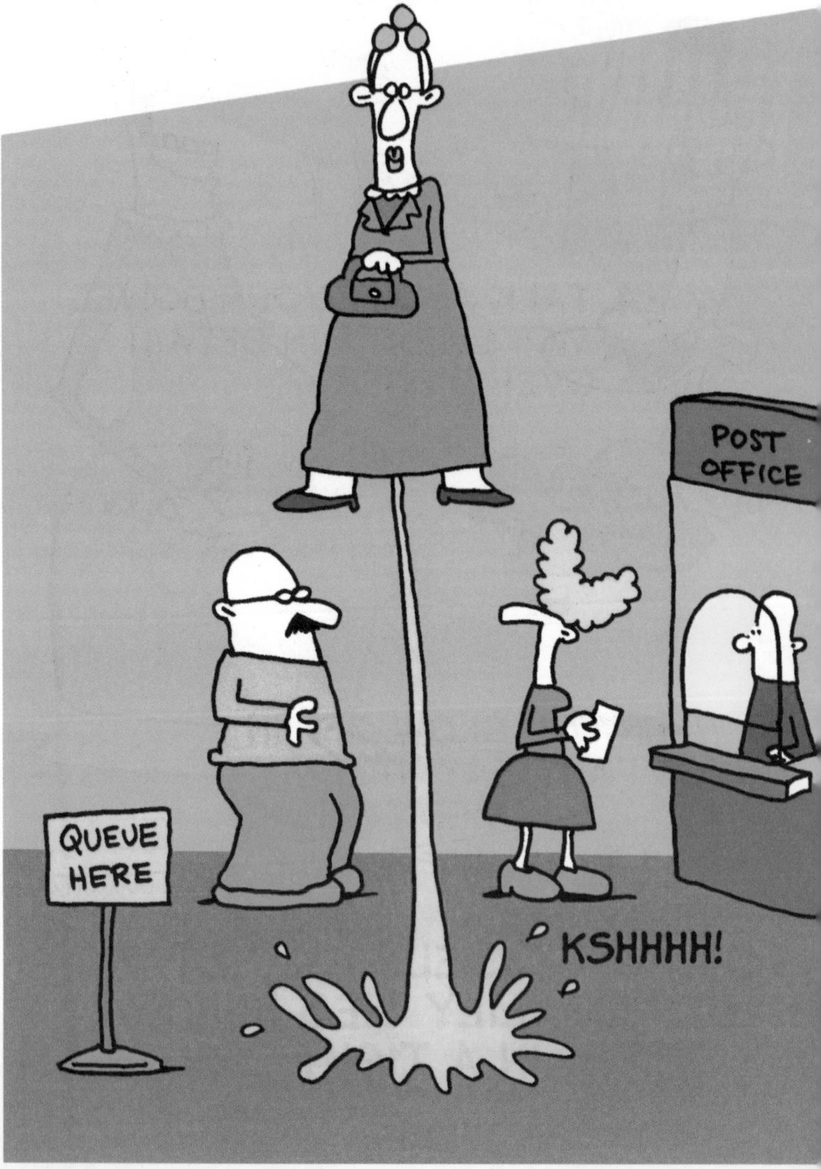
POST OFFICE
QUEUE HERE
KSHHHH!

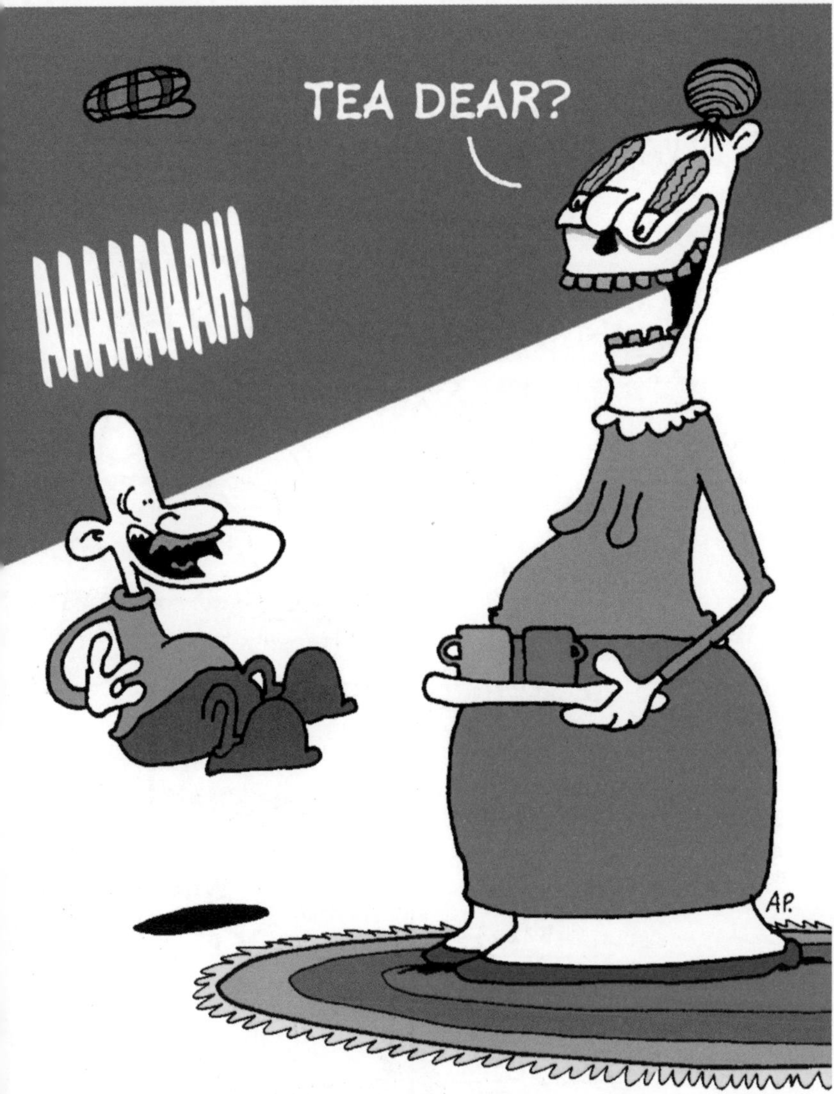
AAAAAAAH!
TEA DEAR?
AP.

TO GIVE HERSELF AN INSTANT FACE LIFT, LILY TIES HER HAIR BACK IN A TIGHT BUN

Ladies! HOW TO FIGHT THE SIGNS OF AGEING!!

1. APPLY WRINKLE CREAM LIBERALLY – PREFERABLY WITH A TROWEL!

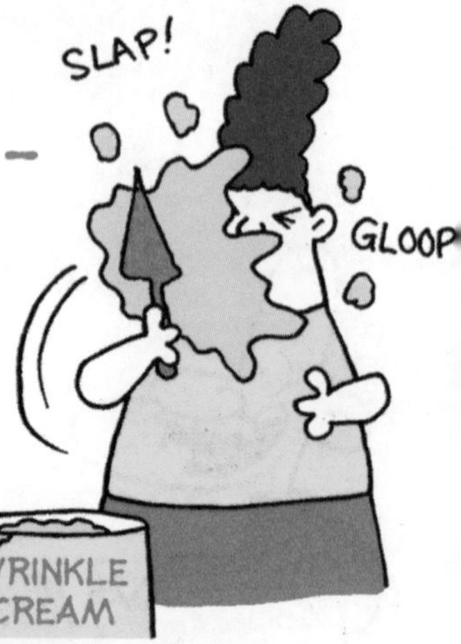
SLAP!
GLOOP
WRINKLE CREAM

2. PREVENT 'OLD LADY TASH' BY SHAVING EVERY HOUR!

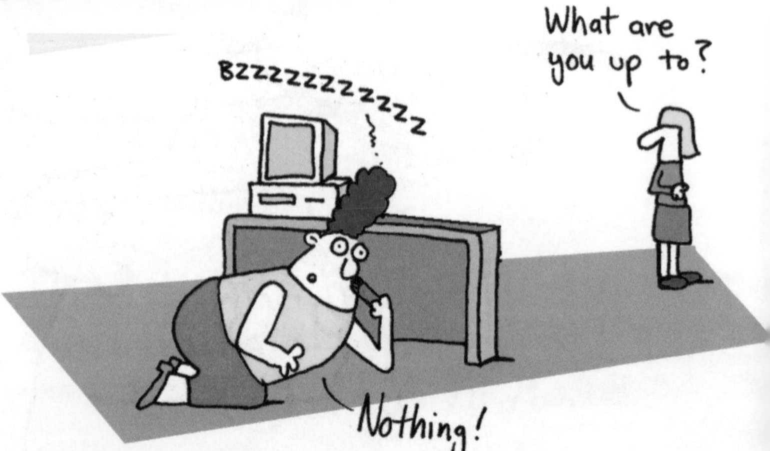
What are you up to?
BZZZZZZZZZZZZ
Nothing!

3. SPRAY REGULARLY WITH EXTRA STRENGTH PERFUME TO MASK THE STENCH OF DECAY!

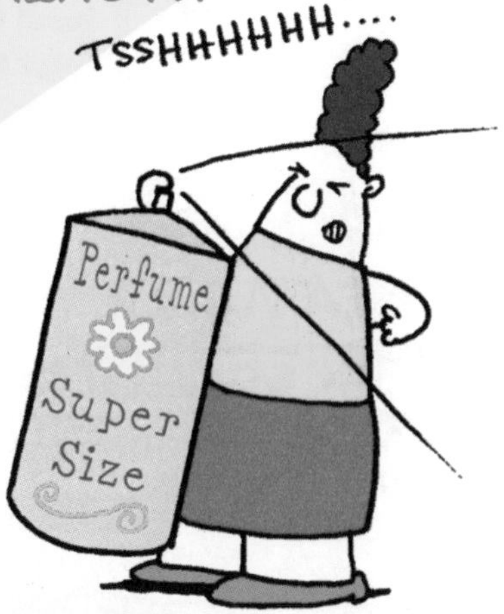
TSSHHHHHH....
Perfume
Super Size

4. RAISE YOUR DROOPY BOOBS BY TYING A COUPLE OF KNOTS IN THEM!

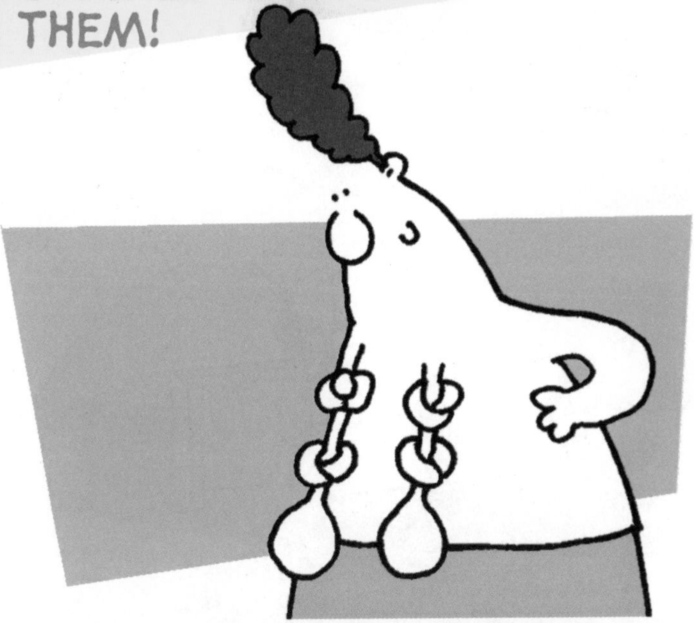

IN HER LATER YEARS, LILY RESORTED TO DESPERATE MEASURES TO BANISH WRINKLES

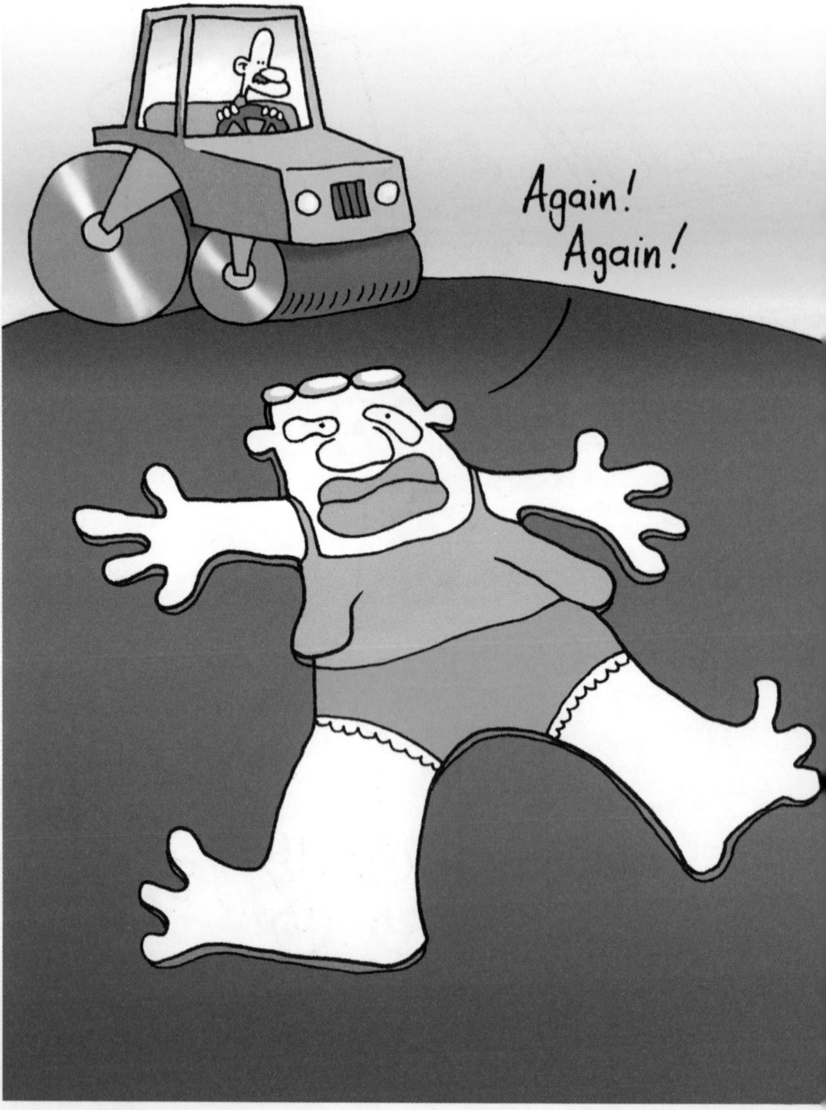
Again! Again!

MAUDE HAD ACTUALLY ASKED THE SURGEON TO TAKE "THE YEARS" OFF HER

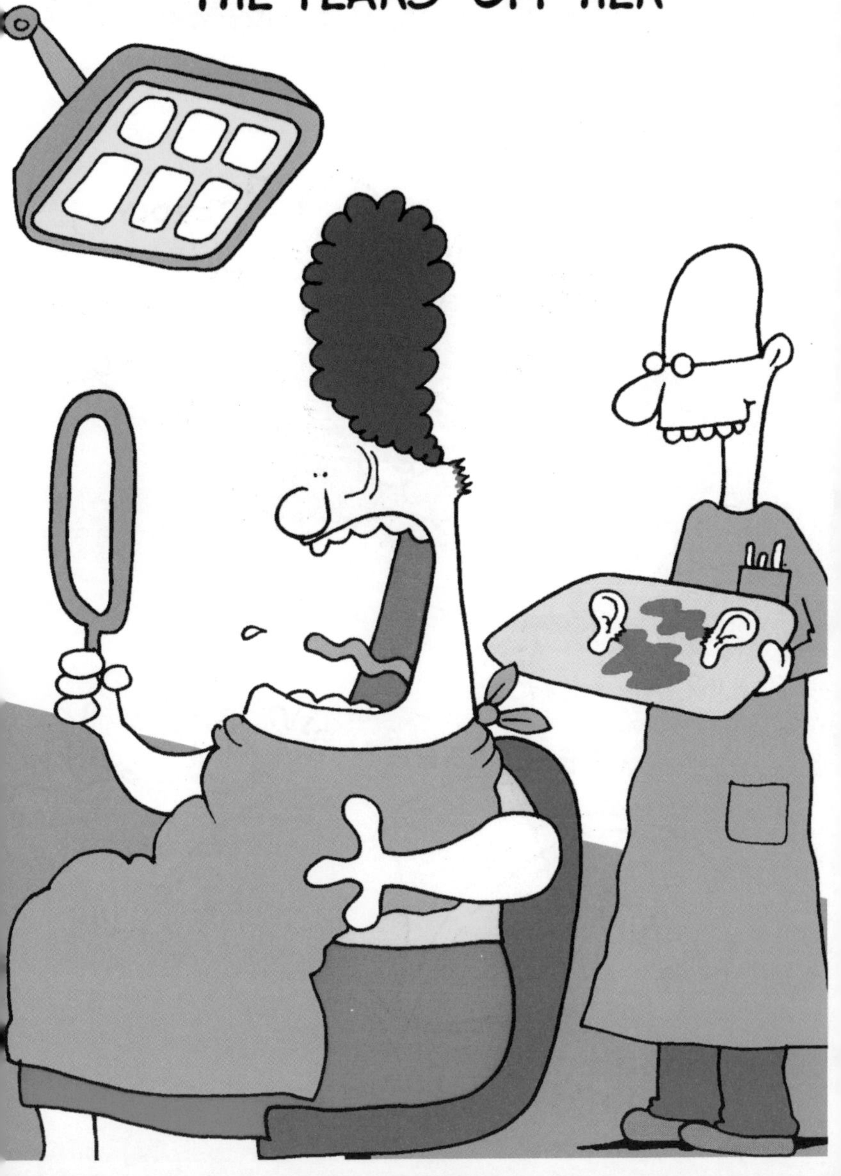

HAVING FUN WITH EXCESS BODY HAIR!

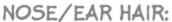

NOSE/EAR HAIR:
PULL TAUT TO MAKE YOUR VERY OWN VIOLIN!

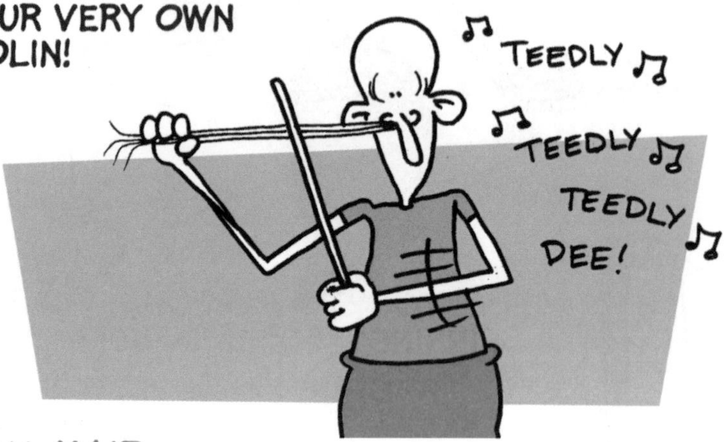
TEEDLY
TEEDLY
TEEDLY
DEE!

BUM HAIR:
CAN BE USED AS A BOUNCING DEVICE!

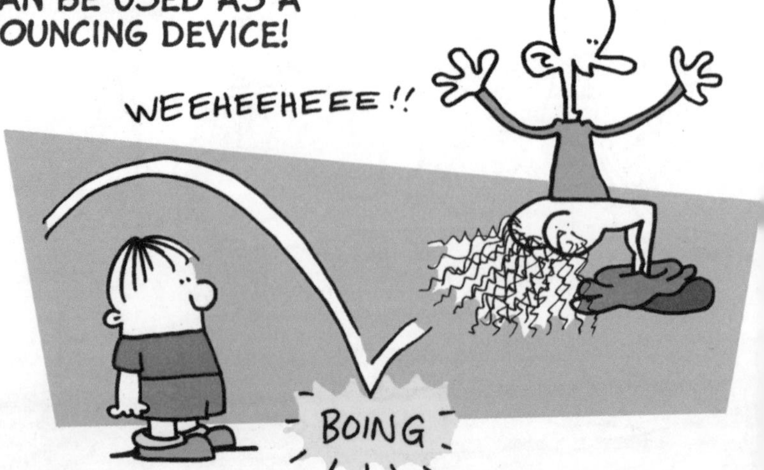
WEEHEEHEEE!!
BOING

EYEBROW HAIR:
SPIN AROUND AND AROUND TO BECOME A HUMAN HELICOPTER!

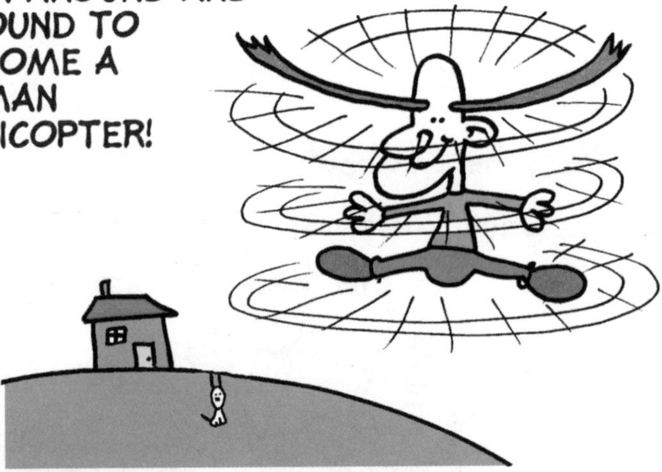

NIPPLE HAIR:
WITH PRACTISE YOU CAN PERFORM YOUR VERY OWN SPINNING TASSEL DANCE!

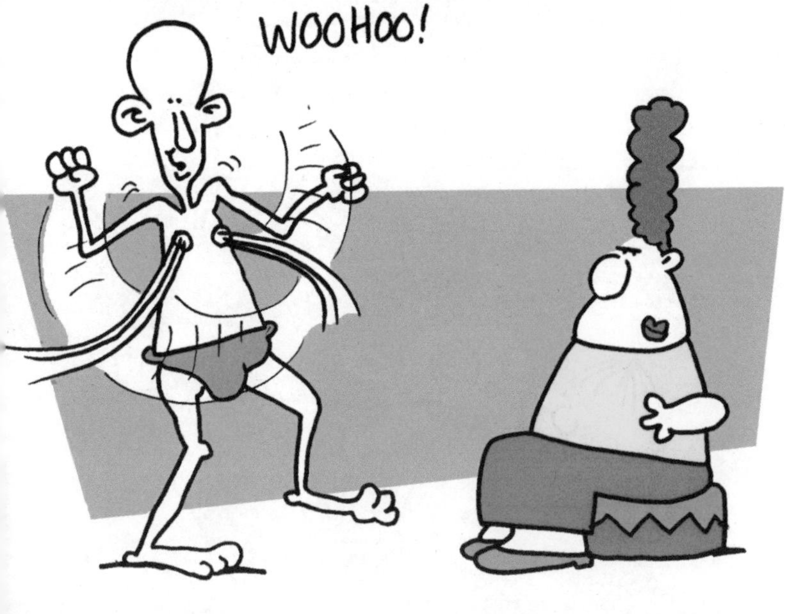
WOOHOO!

MAUDE WAS UPSET BECAUSE SHE HAD LOST HER YOUTH

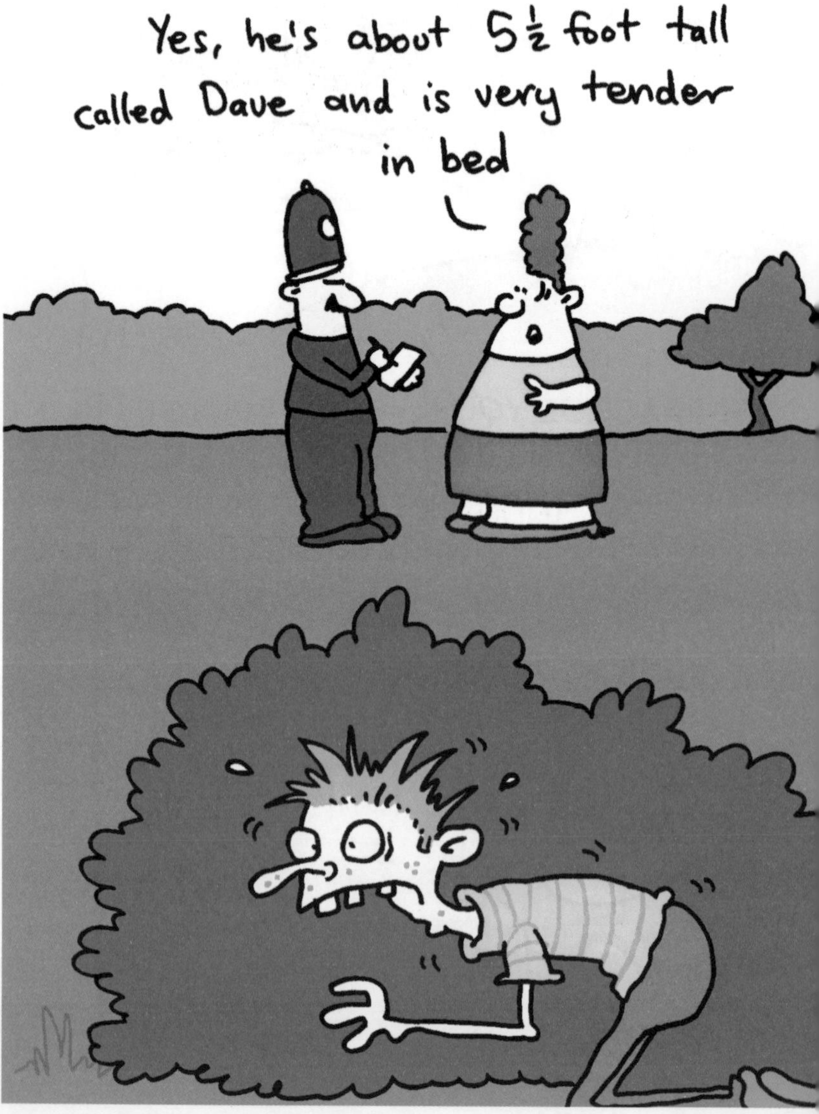
Yes, he's about 5½ foot tall called Dave and is very tender in bed

LILY CATCHES ALF CHECKING OUT ANOTHER WOMAN'S BREASTS

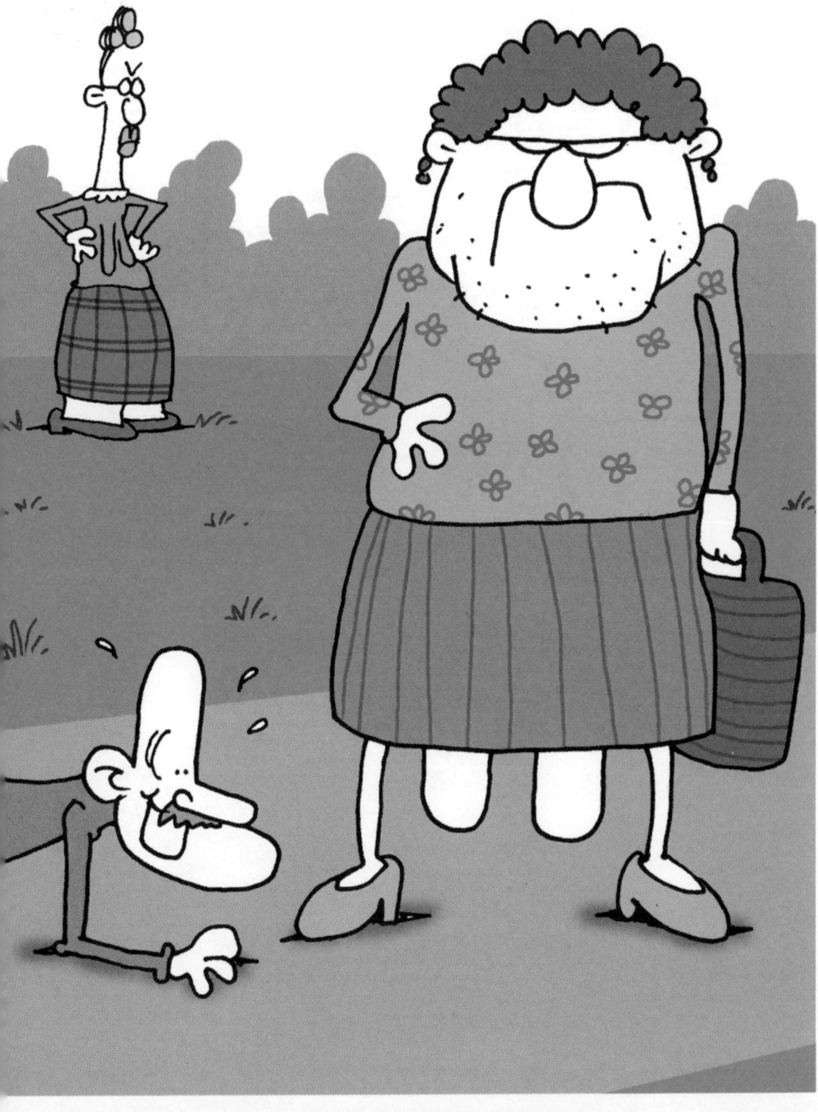

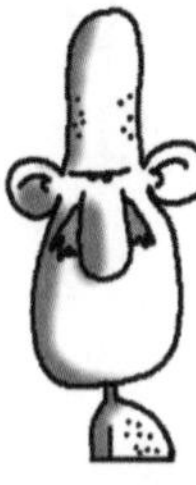

How to stay SEXY as you get older!!!

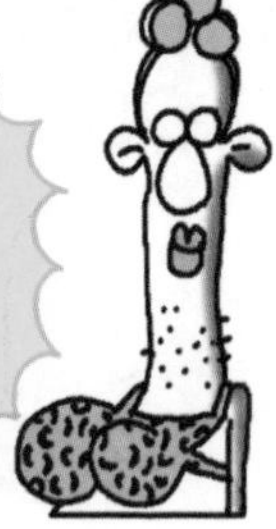

1. LIVEN UP YOUR ZIMMER FRAME WITH ATTRACTIVE LEOPARD SKIN PRINTS!

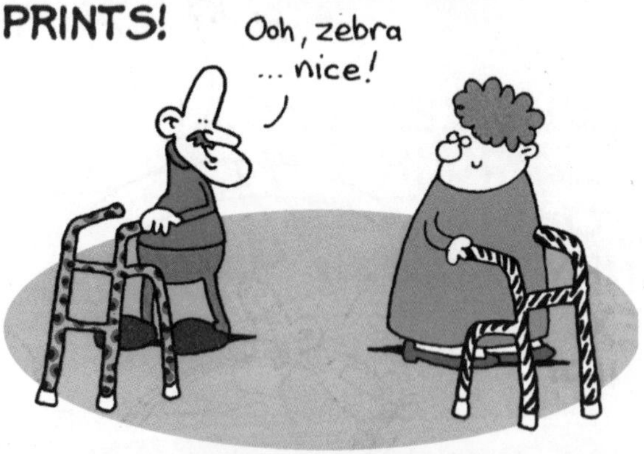
Ooh, zebra ... nice!

2. FILL IN THE GAPS BETWEEN YOUR LIVER SPOTS TO MAKE AN 'ATTRACTIVE' TAN!

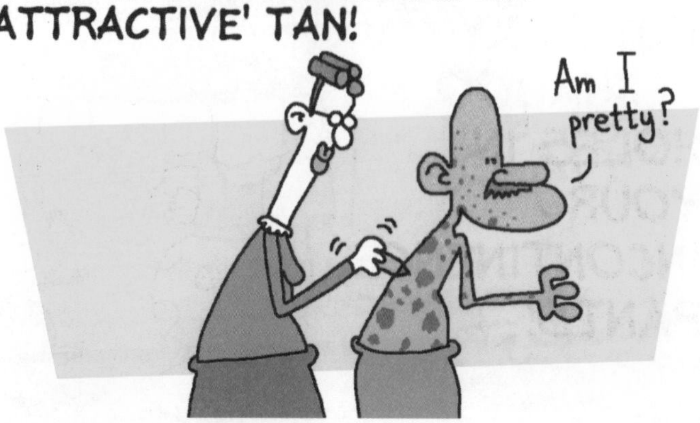
Am I pretty?

3. DON'T LET YOUR TEETH SLIP OUT WHEN YOU'RE SNOGGING!

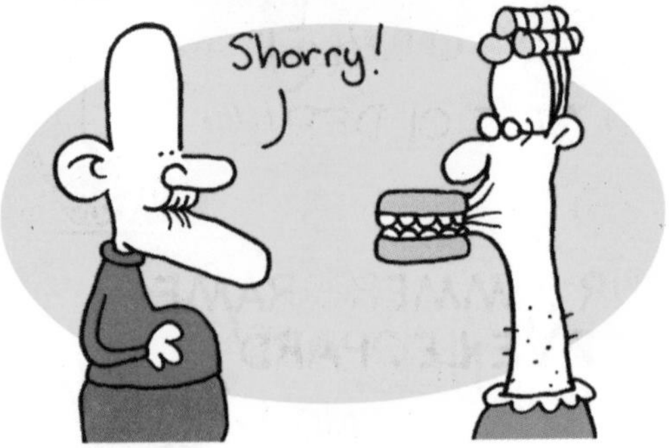
Shorry!

4. FASHION EXCESS NASAL HAIR INTO A KINKY SEX WHIP!

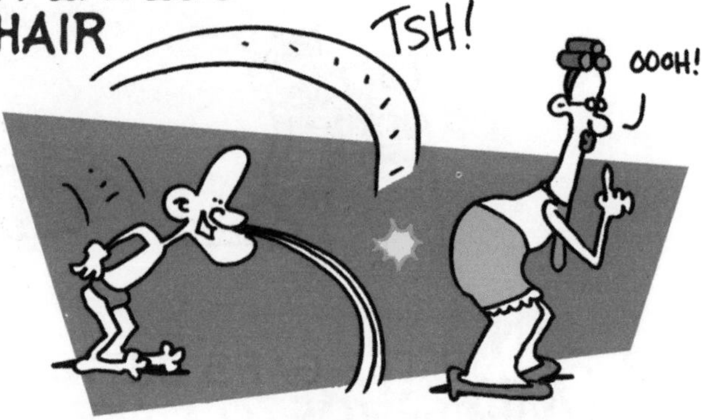
TSH!
OOOH!

5. CUT SEXY PEEKABOO HOLES IN YOUR INCONTINENCE PANTS!

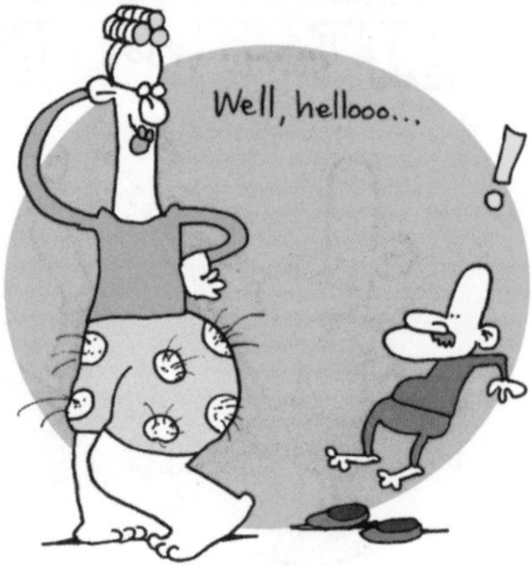
Well, hellooo...
!

HAVING FUN WITH Saggy Testicles!

1. A PLAY TOY FOR CATS!

NO CLAWS! NO CLAWS!!

2. AN EXTENDABLE TAPE MEASURE!

I need some wood THIS long!

3. RETURNABLE GOLF BALL FOR PRACTISING!

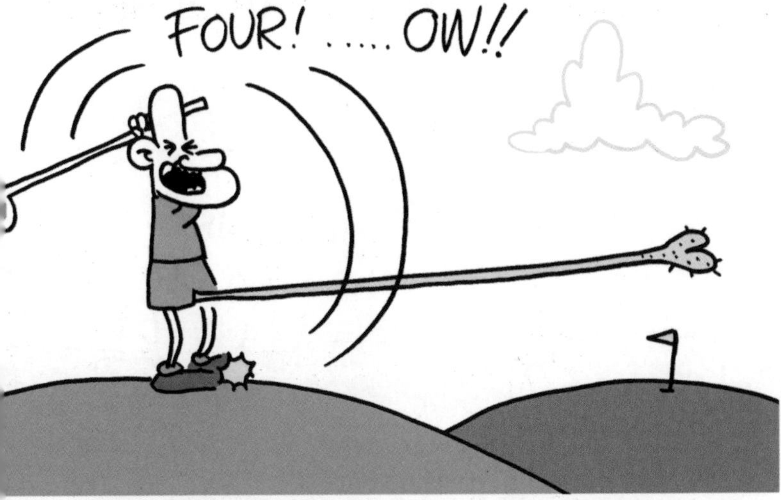
FOUR! .....OW!!

4. TOOTH FLOSS!

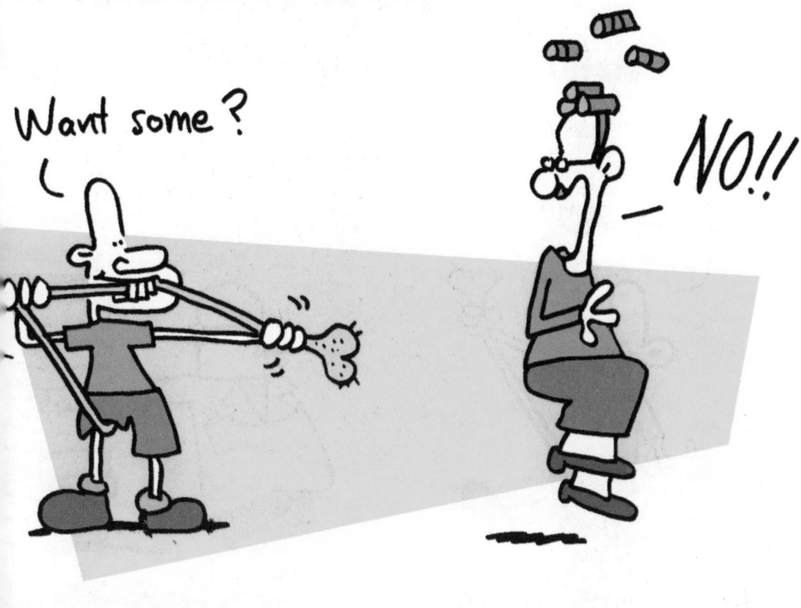
Want some?
NO!!

THE IRONY OF LIFE IS, THE OLDER AND WEAKER YOU GET, THE STRONGER YOUR FARTS BECOM

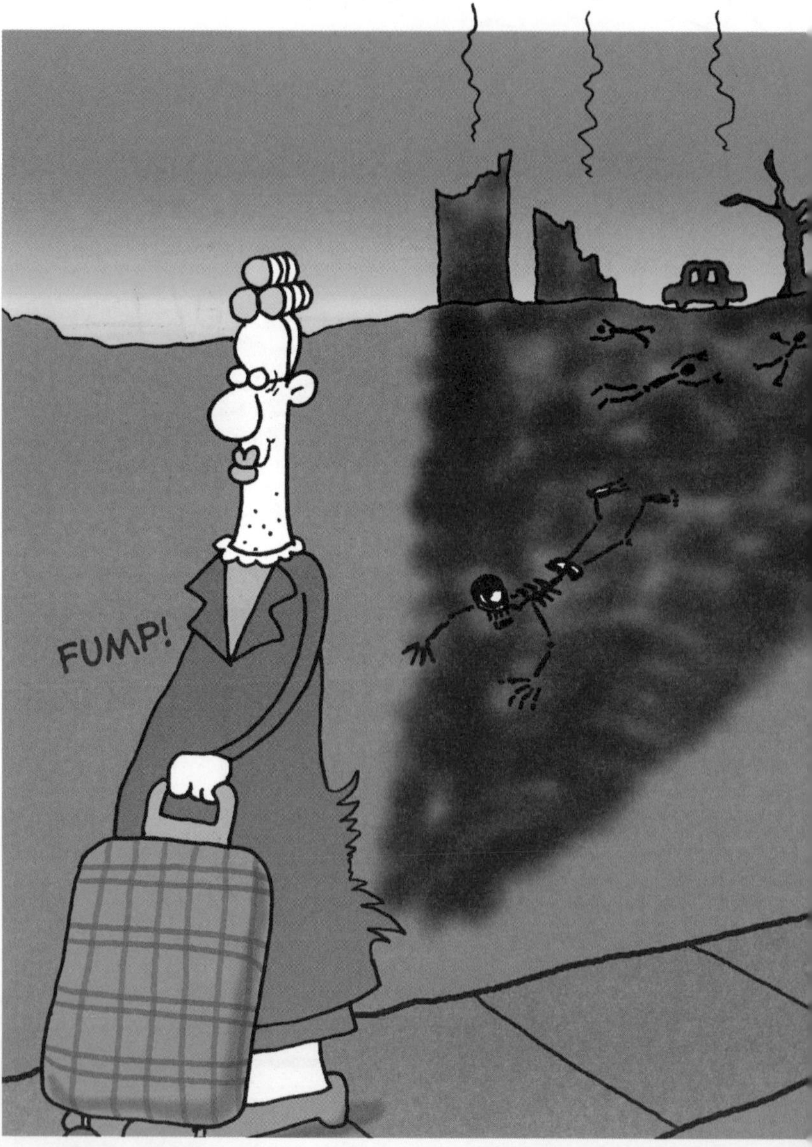
FUMP!

ALF HAD SEVERAL STAINS ON HIS JUMPER SO HE ASKED LILY IF SHE COULD GET THEM OUT

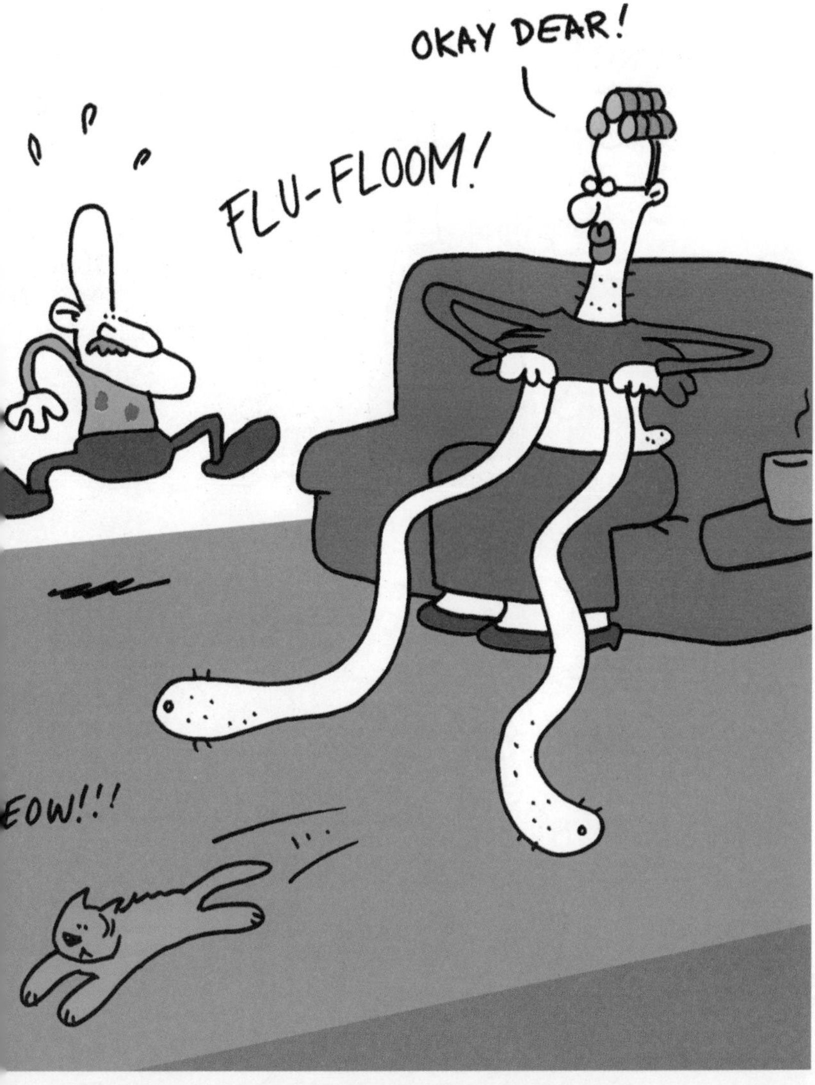
OKAY DEAR!
FLU-FLOOM!
EOW!!!

The PROS and CONS of GETTING OLDER

PRO

YOU DON'T HAVE TO WORRY ABOUT GOING TO THE TOILET

CON

BECAUSE YOU CAN DO IT STRAIGHT INTO YOUR INCONTINENC[E] PANTS

PRO

HAPPINESS IS AN EPISODE OF 'COUNTDOWN'

CON

COUNTDOW[N] ISN'T ON ON A SATURDAY OR SUNDAY

PRO

YOU CAN SHOUT AND MOAN ALL DAY TO PEOPLE

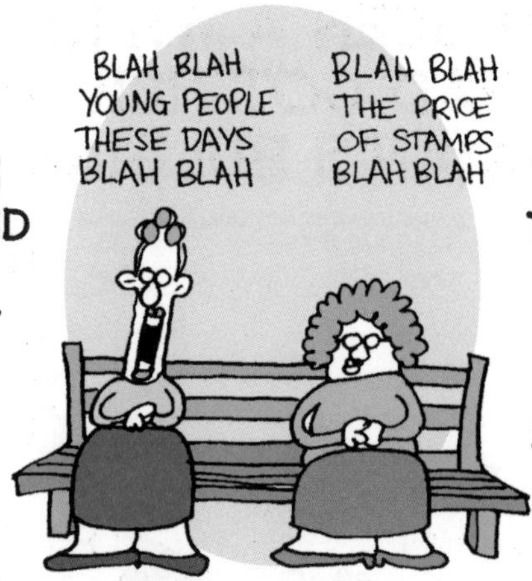
BLAH BLAH YOUNG PEOPLE THESE DAYS BLAH BLAH
BLAH BLAH THE PRICE OF STAMPS BLAH BLAH

CON

YOU HAVE TO LISTEN TO YOUR OLD FRIENDS SHOUTING AND MOANING

PRO

WHEN YOU HAVE A WEE DRINK OF ALCOHOL YOU CAN SAY IT'S 'MEDICINAL'

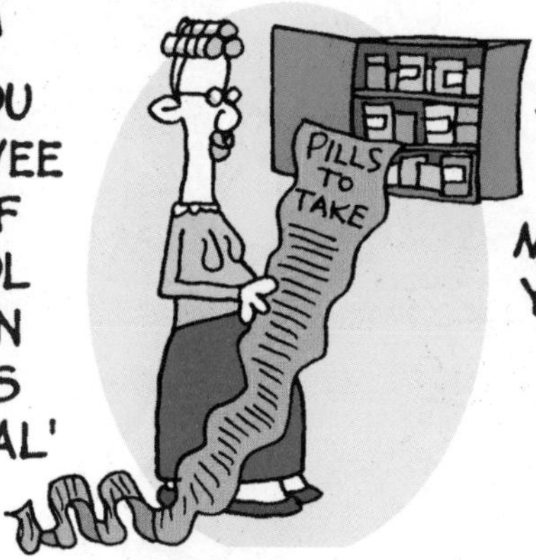
PILLS TO TAKE

CON

YOU'RE ON SO MUCH MEDICATION YOU'RE NOT ALLOWED ALCOHOL!

PRO

YOU DON'T HAVE TO WORRY ABOUT SEX

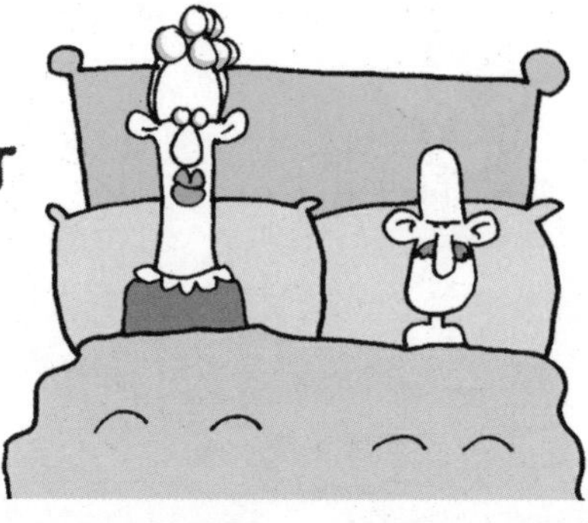

CON

...BECAUSE YOU DON'T GET ANY SEX!

IT HAD BEEN A WHILE SINCE LILY HAD GOT HER HANDS ON A MAN'S BULGING SACK

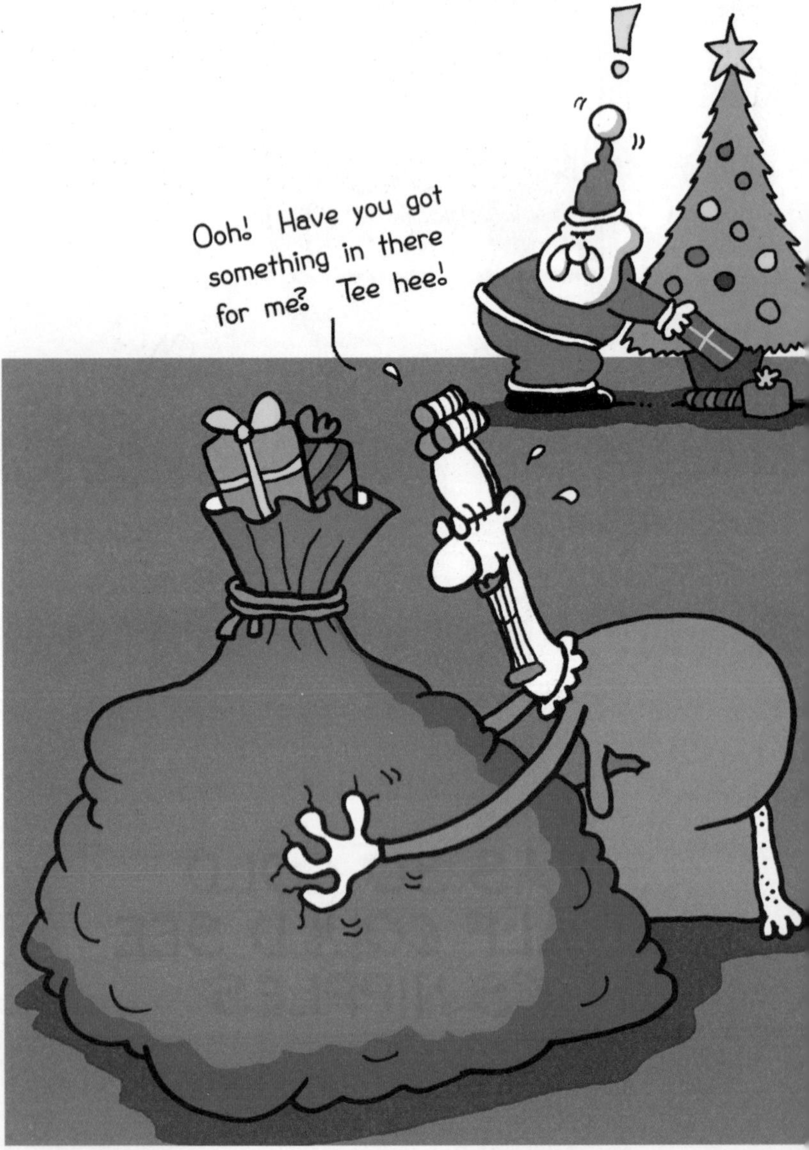
Ooh! Have you got something in there for me? Tee hee!

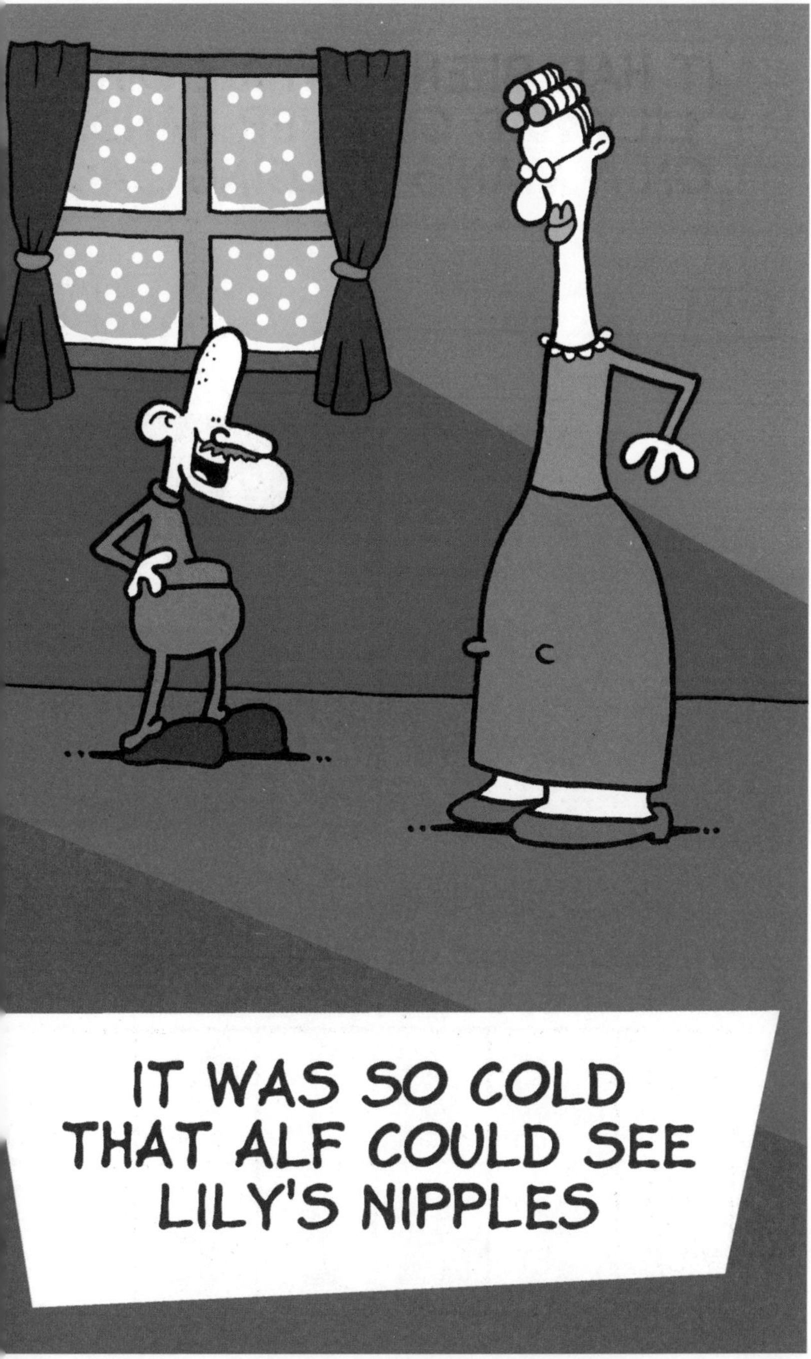
IT WAS SO COLD
THAT ALF COULD SEE
LILY'S NIPPLES

PUZZLES FOR AN OLDIE!
(IN SPECIAL BIG PRINT!)

CROSS WORD!

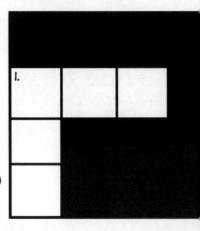

ACROSS
1. THE OPPOSITE OF NEW

DOWN
1. ANOTHER WORD FOR 'PAST IT'

WORD SEARCH!

CAN YOU FIND ANY WORDS IN THE FOLLOWING GRID, DEAR?

S	M	E	L	L	Y
S	E	N	I	L	E

SPOT THE HIP REPLACEMENT!

1.

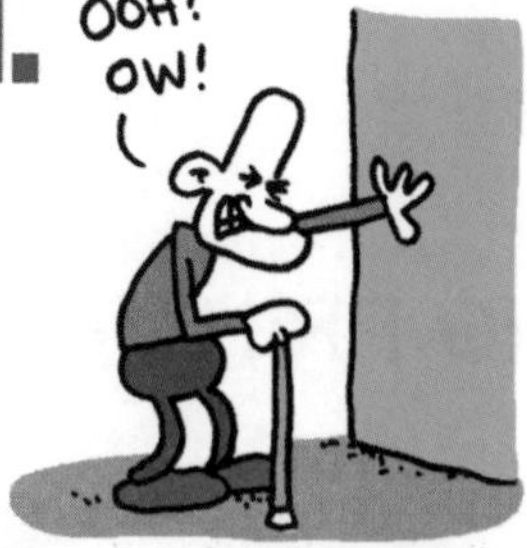
OOH!
OW!

2.

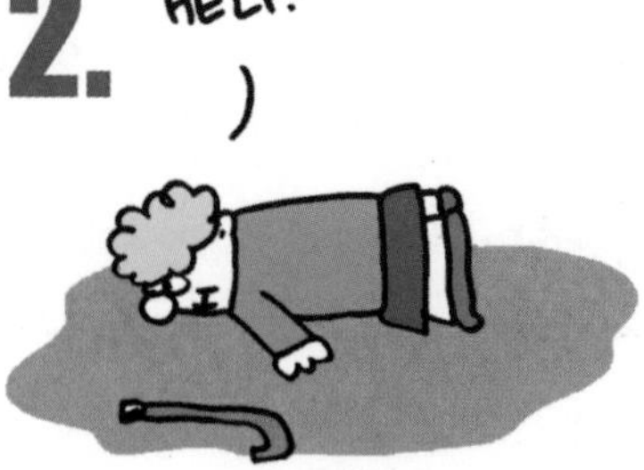
HELP!

3.

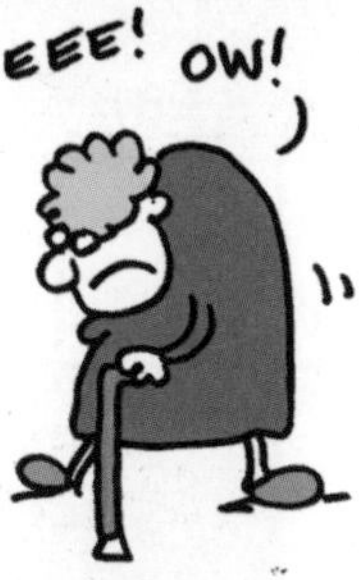
EEE!
OW!

4.

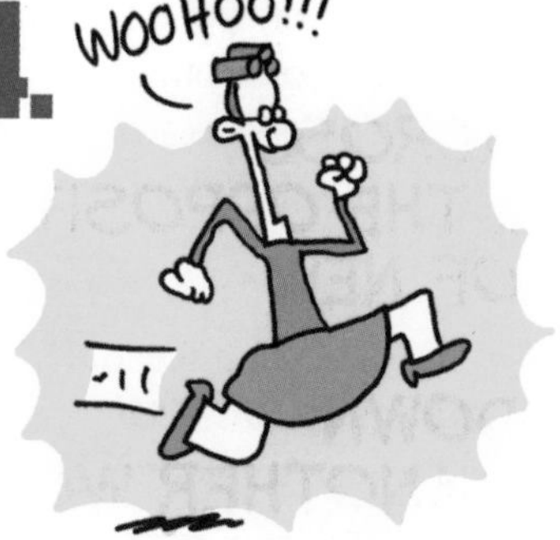
WOOHOO!!!

EYE TEST!

CAN YOU READ THE FOLLOWING OUT LOUD?

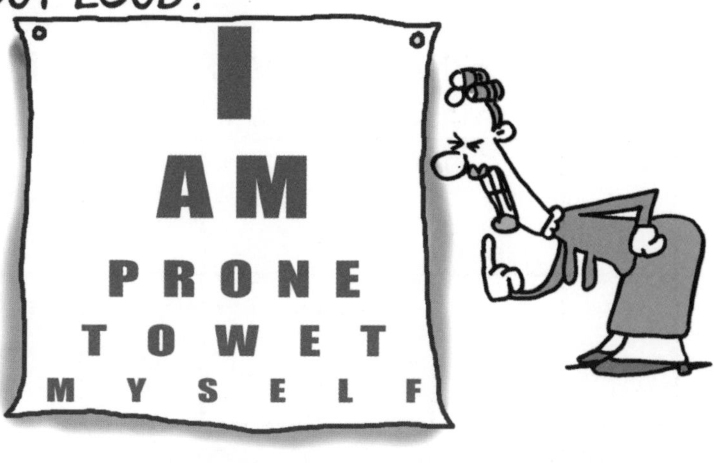
I
AM
P R O N E
T O W E T
M Y S E L F

ODD SQUAD titles available...

		ISBN	P
I Love Beer!	(NEW-hardcover)	1 84161 238 3	£4
I Love Poo!	(NEW-hardcover)	1 84161 240 5	£4
I Love Sex!	(NEW-hardcover)	1 84161 241 3	£4
I Love Wine!	(NEW-hardcover)	1 84161 239 1	£4
The Little Book of Booze		1 84161 138 7	£2
The Little Book of Men		1 84161 093 3	£2
The Little Book of Oldies		1 84161 139 5	£2
The Little Book of Poo		1 84161 096 8	£2
The Little Book of Pumping		1 84161 140 9	£2
The Little Book of Sex		1 84161 095 X	£2
The Little Book of Women		1 84161 094 1	£2
The Little Book of X-Rated Cartoons		1 84161 141 7	£2
Big Poo Handbook	(hardcover)	1 84161 168 9	£7
Sexy Sex Manual	(hardcover)	1 84161 220 0	£7
The Odd Squad Butt Naked		1 84161 190 5	£3
The Odd Squad Gross Out!		1 84161 219 7	£3
The Odd Squad's Saggy Bits		1 84161 218 9	£3
The REAL Kama Sutra		1 84161 103 4	£3
The Odd Squad Volume One		1 85304 936 0	£3

HOW TO ORDER … Please send a cheque/postal order in £ sterling, made payable to 'Ravette Publishing' for the cover price of the books allow the following for postage and packing...

UK & BFPO	60p for the first book & 30p per book thereafte
Europe & Eire	£1.00 for the first book & 50p per book therea
Rest of the world	£1.80 for the first book & 80p per book therea

RAVETTE PUBLISHING   Unit 3, Tristar Centre, Star Road, Partridge Green, West Sussex RH13 8RA

Prices and availability are subject to change without prior notice.